SO-AZV-026

"If you're hungering for SOMETHING MORE THAN COZY, COMFORTABLE, STATUS-QUO RELIGION, Wayne Jacobsen's book is tailor-made for you!"

—Larry Tomczack
People of Destiny International

"This book is REQUIRED READING for anybody I'm working with in church renewal all over the world. I give away cases of them! This is a 'why' book that has been fostered out of years of earnest application and struggle. It is totally authentic. . . ."

—Bob Lanning, Director
School of Church Leadership
University of the Nations

"Wayne Jacobsen tells us what's wrong with the church—but many have done that. He goes on to present A VISION OF WHAT TRUE CHRISTIANITY IS ALL ABOUT and then inspires us to get on board. His vision for the church is something everyone interested in true fellowship should read."

—Terry C. Muck
Associate Professor of Religion
Austin Presbyterian Theological
Seminary

"In *A Passion for God's Presence*, Wayne Jacobsen PEELS AWAY THE SUPERFICIAL GILDING that supposedly indicates the church's prosperity, but which in reality is a thin veneer covering over the poverty WHEREIN GLITTER SUBSTITUTES FOR GODLINESS.

—Jerry Horner
Dean, College of Theology and
Ministry
Regent University

This book is AN UNABASHED INVITATION TO STOP TRYING TO MAKE GOD FIT INTO OUR LIVES, AND MAKE OUR LIVES FIT GOD'S UNEARTHLY SCHEME."

—Marshall Shelley
Editor, *Leadership*

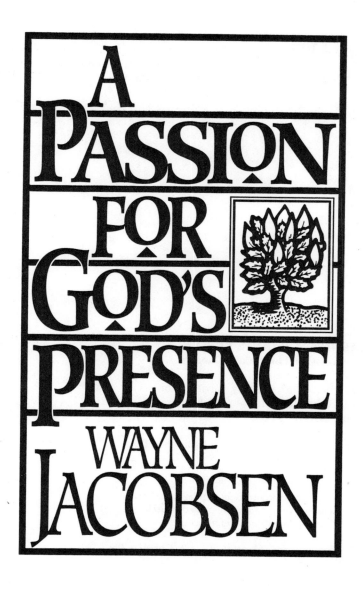

A PASSION FOR GOD'S PRESENCE

WAYNE JACOBSEN

HARVEST HOUSE PUBLISHERS
Eugene, Oregon 97402

Verses marked NIV are taken from the Holy Bible, New International Version, Copyright © 1978 by the New York International Bible Society. Used by permission of Zondervan Bible Publishers.

A PASSION FOR GOD'S PRESENCE
Formerly titled **The Naked Church**

Copyright © 1987, 1991 by Wayne Jacobsen
Published by Harvest House Publishers
Eugene, Oregon 97402

Library of Congress Cataloging-in-Publication Data

Jacobsen, Wayne.
    [Naked church]
    A passion for God's presence / Wayne Jacobsen.
    Previously published as: The naked church.
    Includes bibliographical references.
    ISBN 0-89081-916-5
    1. Christianity—20th century.   2. Christian life—1960-
  I. Title.
BR121.2.J274   1991
262'.001'7—dc20   91-10338
                                             CIP

All rights reserved. No portion of this book may be reproduced in any form without the written permission of the Publisher.

Printed in the United States of America.

For the hurting,
the hungry,
the brave,
who have refused to settle
for anything short of God's fullness
which he promised us in Christ Jesus, his Son,
despite any obstacle or discouragement
of man or circumstance!

Contents

Foreword

Authentic Christianity is not merely a meeting—it is a way of life born of an intimate relationship with Jesus Christ. Out of that relationship the early believers "devoted themselves to the apostles' teaching and to fellowship, to the breaking of bread and to prayer" (Acts 2:42). The power of Christ shaped their lifestyles and called them to share their vibrant faith from "house to house."

As judgment on our society increases and pressure mounts, believers will no longer be able to survive by mere participation in a Bible study, prayer-and-praise meeting, para-church organization, evangelistic ministry, or traditional service. As good as these involvements may be, alone they just won't be sufficient.

Christians increasingly need to cultivate an ever-deepening relationship with God. Not in theory but in reality. They must learn to hear his voice and rely on his grace, refusing every substitute for the active presence of God in their daily lives.

In this day God is raising up a generation of people who are committed to having a passion for his presence, and to sharing that life together as a community . . . a spiritual family. They are realizing their need to be joined to brothers and sisters who share an all-consuming commitment to follow Jesus and to be a living expression of the body of Christ.

God's intention for this people in these crises times of judgment is that we find our place in a church that's committed to New Testament principle and practice. This isn't optional—it's essential. Our other activities cannot interfere with our responsibility to be active with other believers in a local church built on biblical foundations and committed to nurturing his presence.

Truly, there has never been a day like this in the history of the church. Judgment has begun. Difficult challenges await us. Yet after centuries of darkness and paralysis in the body of Christ, the Holy Spirit is working at an accelerated pace to prepare a bride for the return of her Bridegroom. God's original intention "to present her to himself as a radiant church, without stain or wrinkle or any other blemish" (Ephesians 5:27) is not mere wishful thinking. It is becoming more of a reality with each passing day, and God wants you to be a part of that bride.

As we respond to God and commit ourselves to the restoration of intimacy in our own relationship with God, and as we join together to see him restore that sleeping giant known as the church, we'll understand the shout that Jesus will give when he returns (1 Thessalonians 4:16). Surely excitement will explode in his heart as he rends the heavens to receive his bride—his glorious church—restored to his original intentions, fulfilling every one of his purposes.

Would we want to present him with anything less?

—Larry Tomczack
People of Destiny
International

Acknowledgments

Many friendships and conversations of days past have helped to shape my life and the ideas contained in this book. It would be impossible to thank all the people involved, but I especially want to express my heartfelt appreciation for those whose contributions have been deep and enduring:

To Sara, my wife, who has shared my hunger for God and with whom I have tasted the beauty and fullness of life in Christ.

To the people of a church affectionately called Savior's, for accepting the challenge of pursuingthe presence of Jesus, looking to please him above themselves, and for giving me the time to write this book. Particularly I want to note the contributions of Mark Condie, my copastor, with whom I have hammered out the truths in this book and how they apply to everyday living.

To my father of flesh and faith, Gene Jacobsen, who walks more closely with God than anyone I know, and my mother, Jo, for investing her life in mine.

To two of my past pastors, Dr. Robert "Brother Bob" Stamps and Roger Whitlow, for showing me what God is like and what it means to follow him.

To the late Dr. Clyde Kilby of Wheaton College, whose encouragement for me to keep writing sustained me through many a difficulty.

To friends and critics who have helped with the manuscript itself: Elaine Roberts (my longtime editor on far more projects than this), Ron Vincent, Dave Coleman, and my Christian Writer's Critique Group.

To Eileen Mason and Bill Jensen of Harvest House, whose suggestions brought this work into focus and made it available to you.

PASSION
FOR
GOD'S
PRESENCE

1

The Day the Journey Started

If anyone would come after me,
he must deny himself and take up
his cross and follow me.
—Matthew 16:24

I can't say I was totally unsuspecting when the moment finally came. It had stalked me for months, like a patient lion.

But that was clearer by hindsight, since at the time I kept suppressing the doubts I had about the effectiveness of American Christianity. I chased the thoughts away, avoiding the conclusions and the actions they would compel me to make. I threw myself headlong into the busyness and pressing concerns of professional ministry. That's why I was still surprised when the final assault was launched.

It happened at midmorning while I was distracted by a pile of paperwork. Thoughts I had ignored individually over the past few months now marched across my mind in rank. I whirled my padded chair away from the cluttered desk, leaned back, and sighed. Through my full-length window I gazed on a fluorescent purple azalea in the courtyard. It was in full bloom, regal in the spring sunlight—a promise, I hoped, of a favorable outcome to this moment of conflict.

Why do we try so hard to avoid the inevitable? Maybe we think that nothing really is inevitable, or that if it is we can at least postpone it. Either way, our attitude only makes life harder on us and the people around us. When the moment came that April morning, it was far less emotional than I had imagined. I remember looking at the azalea and chuckling. It was such a simple conclusion, one made without blinding light or overwhelming guilt.

My current experience with church ministry matched neither the hunger that churned so deep within me nor what I perceived to be the challenge of Scripture. In one moment all my excuses were swept away by a mass of evidence I could no longer ignore. When I looked for whys I kept coming to the same conclusion: Our application of contemporary Christianity was deeply inadequate. I knew it wasn't the people; those I worked with loved the Lord deeply. I knew it wasn't a disregard for Scripture; we believed it wholeheartedly. I knew it wasn't a lack of knowledge; I already knew far more than I was living out at the time.

But when I looked at how church ministry operated, I saw how high a priority it places on safety and routine. At the cost of distracting people from personal intimacy with Jesus, it clings to the status quo. It placates the lukewarm and cools the zealous. It has not led us to the fullness of Jesus' life but rather lured us away.

"That's it!" I said aloud. "I'm going to find a Christianity as powerful as the one I have read about in Acts, no matter what!" That may have sounded gallant, but it wasn't. The status quo became so distasteful to me that if I were wrong and this really was all there could be to church life, then I did not want to spend the rest of my life in pastoral ministry.

Whenever I've shared this moment with people, they invariably ask what was wrong with that church. Nothing! It was (and still is) one of the finest I know of, and I can't recommend a better church anywhere. It is a spiritually vital church in central California with statistics that would make any church-growth expert drool with delight.

Nor was I frustrated with my part in it. I served a pastor whose spiritual life I admired, and still do. We share the same theological orientation and hunger to see people touched with the life of Jesus. Only four years out of college, I taught classes regularly numbering in the hundreds, administered a budget in excess of a half-million dollars, and could rarely walk into a store without being recognized. I owned a home and two cars and drew a significant salary in a traditionally underpaid occupation. I was just beginning to break into print with my free-lance writing, and I was in the middle of the charismatic-evangelical groundswell of the late 1970's.

I loved it all until certain Scriptures started nagging at me. Yes, I fought back, rationalizing when I could and getting help from others when I couldn't. It seems few people really believe that the church in Acts is a pragmatic model for us today, and everyone has reasons why. But my "whys" were wearing thin. I began to see my spiritual life in unmitigated comparison to the Word, and I felt naked.

I'm not sure what finally did it. That final week had not been particularly distinctive. It might have been the nine-year-old girl who fought asthma for every breath she took in spite of our fervent prayers for healing. Maybe it was the young woman trapped in emotional bondage because of abuse in her childhood, desperately wanting to be free and finding no one who could take the time to make the Christianity we spoke of real for her. Or it might have been the two believers I was trying to reconcile who could not even speak to each other. And then again it could have been that one more request stacked on my desk from someone who needed a "word from Wayne" to get through the day.

Most likely it wasn't any one of these, but the weight of them all and countless other situations like them. But these four circumstances illustrate the concerns that nagged me most.

I couldn't reconcile God's promises of healing with the hit-and-miss results I witnessed. The early church was alive with a power I had witnessed early in the charismatic renewal but had seen diminish as its churches grew larger and its message more palatable to the culture.

I couldn't reconcile the love of God with hurting people who slipped through the cracks of our program or neatly formulated creed. The young woman trapped in emotional bondage had been in many churches over a seven-year period but was not finding freedom. Psychiatry had been unable to help, telling her to function as best she could until she needed to be institutionalized. The strong can shoulder their way in anywhere, but who was defending the weak and seeking out the strays?

I couldn't reconcile our challenge to self-sacrificing love with the pettiness, gossip, and manipulation that characterized so many church relationships.

And I couldn't reconcile Jesus' words for leaders to be the servants of all when I basked in the notoriety and physical comfort that pastoral ministry had brought me. Far from being a living example of what it means to be a disciple, I had merely become the figment of people's imagination. The "Wayne" they visualized was different from the one I lived with, not because I harbored secret sins, but because no one knew the real me. I was Wayne the "gifted teacher" or "wise counselor," and not simply a believer with hurts and joys like everyone else. And what scared me most was that I liked it that way!

If I were convinced that these examples are only a few chinks in an otherwise-productive system, I would not be so deeply troubled. But they are not. They result from a system that puts more credibility in its own efforts than on the power of God, and its toll is taken in personal lives. It is time for someone to stand up and say something even if it would be more fun to stay in the stands and cheer with everyone else. But when you realize that it is no game, that lives are being devoured in lion-sized bites, how can you go on cheering?

This doesn't mean that our present system has never helped anyone, nor should these comments be construed as a sweeping condemnation of all people involved in such structures. I know many people in the system who enjoy a very deep relationship with the Lord. Though I am grateful for them, they are the exceptions. Many more people—those not so fortunate or so strong—have been alienated from God by the very structure that should convey his love.

I turned back from the azalea and scanned the piles of papers on my desk and my open Bible perched on the front-left corner. The battle was over: My days in the system were numbered. That day eventually cost me my staff position, though not because I was asked to resign nor because I did so as a martyr. I had no desire to be divisive. My pastor proved to be my friend, caring deeply about my struggles even though we both knew that our obedience lay down different paths. God provided a new fellowship that shared my hunger to discover what he wanted to do in his church without the rigors of tradition or the bondages of institutional structure. But I soon discovered that geography was not the only thing God wanted to change in my life. Eight months after I had assumed my new pastorate I came to another fork in the road in an encounter far more emotional than the one described above. In my journal I titled it "The End of Comfortable Christianity." Church structures were only the branches and leaves of the problems I struggled with; now I saw the roots—the appetites within. My idealism was tested by a challenge to personal change. My obedience lay not in changing other people but in my own surrender to the will of God.

No longer could I appease my flesh in the name of spirituality. No longer could I compete for the affection and affirmation of people. I had to give up the trappings to which I had become accustomed and instead clothe myself in Christ Jesus in a far more painful way than I had imagined. Only then did I truly understand the cost of the decision I had made that morning as the azalea looked on. Yet I have never regretted it, for I have discovered just how real Jesus can become in the joy of hammering out his desires for my life.

What follows is what I have discovered seven years into the journey. These are the words of a traveler, for I have not yet arrived at my destination. Growing in intimacy is a lifelong process, and there are still promises ahead that I have not reached. But I'm closer now than when I began. My prayer is that this book can encourage other travelers already on the road, and challenge some others to begin.

To undertake the journey, however, we must commit to loving Jesus more than anything else in the world and be willing to reject whatever keeps us at arm's length from the glory of his presence. On that April morning I began a search for a vital Christian experience, a Christianity that is real for every person who wants it. Without such an experience the church is naked no matter how extensive its programs or ornate its buildings.

I know these words are challenging, but this is no diatribe; it is a confessional. Regarding the abuses and excesses I address, I have been a victim of all and a perpetrator of most. These are not words of rebellion but of repentance and reformation.

Not long ago I heard of a pastor caught in the very act of adultery. As I passed that choice morsel of gossip to a college friend of mine, I expected him to break out with the same righteous indignation that churned in me. Instead he began to cry and pray, "My God, forgive us for offending your Son." That's an attitude we all need. Instead of finger-pointing at others or rising to our own defense, we need to take a careful look and repent. Have we forced Christianity into a religious system unbefitting a personal relationship with the Lord of Glory? And if we have, can we leave it for something far more real, even though it costs us greatly?

I commend the journey to you, not because it is full of fun and quick success but because it is what Scripture calls us to and because we have little choice as servants except to obey the will of the Master. But this doesn't mean that it isn't worth the going. What I've found on the way answers the deepest hungers of my heart. Nothing compares to living every day reconciled with God and filled with his presence. It is a walk of joy and glory far exceeding any other adventure you'll ever find.

What else is there?

2

Rise Up and Walk?

The prophets prophesy lies,
the priests rule by their own authority,
and my people love it this way.
But what will you do in the end?
—Jeremiah 5:31

America has begun a spiritual awakening. Faith
and hope are being restored. Americans are turning
back to God. Church attendance is up. Audiences
for religious books and broadcasts are growing. In
college campuses, students have stopped shunning
religion and started going to church.[1]

Impressive statement, isn't it? And all the more so when we
realize that it was said by an incumbent President of the
United States. This was Ronald Reagan's assessment in 1984
of the spiritual temper of America as he addressed a conven-
tion of evangelicals.

He is certainly not alone in his jubilation. Everywhere we
look in the 80's we seem to see the church recovering visibility
after a notable decline in the 50's and 60's. The evidence seems
overwhelming.

• Ninety-five percent of Americans believe in God and 81
percent consider themselves religious.[2] Seventy-six percent say they attend church sometimes during the year
and 87 percent say they pray sometime during their daily
lives.[3]

• Thirty-seven billion dollars was given to churches and
religious organizations in 1985.[4] In 1986, the top seven
media evangelists alone took in more than 750 million
dollars.[5]

11

- At last count 138,452,614 people were on the church rolls of America and Canada.[6] Thousands of churches are spread all across the world today and missionaries are in virtually every corner of the globe. Superchurches, those numbering more than 1000 people, dot our cities, and one in South Korea grows beyond half a million.
- Christianity even boasts its own powerful and influential media—four national TV networks and hundreds of local TV and radio stations. Magazine and book publishers abound.
- *Time* magazine may have called 1976 the Year of the Evangelical, but the church's political influence has only strengthened in the 80's. Both major political parties openly courted the evangelical vote in 1984.

You would think we're in the middle of a great revival, and that's exactly what Pat Robertson, head of the Christian Broadcasting Network, concluded at Amsterdam '83, an international gathering of evangelists.

> I wouldn't wish to exchange this moment for any other time in the history of mankind. . . . In these days ahead, I believe that it will truly be said of the Church of the Lord Jesus Christ, "This is her finest hour."[7]

A Closer Look

In the face of such success and accolades, one would have to be foolish to even suggest that the church is naked. Or would he? While Pat Robertson may be accurate from a worldwide perspective, with revival reports coming in from China, Africa, and behind the Iron Curtain, a closer look at the church in the West might yield a different conclusion. Not everyone is as impressed with the state of American Christianity.

Chuck Colson is deeply concerned:

> The church has been brought into the same value system [as the world]: fame, success, materialism

and celebrity. We watch the leading churches and the leading Christians for our cues. We want to emulate the best-known preachers with the biggest sanctuaries and the grandest edifices. Preoccupation with these values has perverted the church's message.[8]

Mr. Colson saw something hidden behind the impressive statistics I listed earlier. Selected statistics can accentuate the positive while ignoring the hurts. It's easy to write up the four people who got healed at the last healing service and ignore the 400 who walked away unhealed, feeling that God has somehow singled them out for rejection.

Here is another list of facts about American Christianity. Don't they make Chuck Colson's conclusion a bit more credible?

- Though 95 percent of Americans believe in God, a Gallup poll also found that only 12 percent of the populace "could be considered deeply and highly spiritually committed." Between 8 and 13 percent are engaged in evangelism and only 3 to 5 percent use spiritual gifts.[9] One maxim given to church leaders is that 10 percent of the people will do 90 percent of the work, while the rest come along for the ride.

- Dare we ask if our billion-dollar industry is merchandising the gospel with a vengeance unknown since Jesus drove the money-changers from the temple? Many Christian suppliers are owned by non-Christian corporations and function with greater zeal for profits than for ministry. I know a recording artist who was denied the opportunity to sing in jails by his producer because "it won't sell records."

- Isn't something wrong when the musicians of the body of Christ peddle their gifts for 15 dollars a seat, and then only in large cities where there are enough people to make the trip worthwhile? Is it any different when a speaker charges a six-dollar entrance fee to share what he's learned about family life?

- From an interview question posed by *Leadership* magazine: "Here are two stark figures from the *World Christian*

Encyclopedia on conversions 1970-1980: The United States —with all its evangelism programs, training seminars, books, crusades and media ministries—showed a net loss (minus 595,900), while over the same decade the Soviet Union saw a net gain of 164,182 [people]. What are we doing wrong?"[10]

- Immorality and financial impropriety on the part of our Christian leaders are daily fodder for the secular press. Our television celebrities think nothing of purchasing 50,000-dollar cars and large homes in our nation's resort cities. They board their private jets even as their videotapes beg for finances to keep the ministry going. In my own city in a six-month period, one minister was caught in the act of adultery and another was sentenced for tax fraud. His excessive salary (4000 dollars per week) and spending (1200 dollars for hair styling and 2700 dollars for massage parlors in Los Angeles) were front-page news. Both pastors continue in active ministry today.

- The same problems that plague society also flourish in the church. "The late George Gallup, Sr. discovered a most bewildering paradox: religious interest is growing at an unprecedented rate, he said, but so is immoral behavior. Gallup's poll revealed 'little difference between those who go to church and those who don't.' "[11] Divorce and promiscuity abound. Businessmen fudge on their taxes, excusing themselves with "it's the only way to survive."

- A friend of mine tried out recently for the choir of one of Southern California's better-known churches. His excitement at having passed the audition was quickly squashed by the reality he encountered in the choir room. Off-color jokes and backbiting against others in the choir abounded. He eventually quit and floundered for months in his spiritual experience, alienated by the hypocrisy he found at what he thought was one of the best churches that America had to offer.

- There's more truth than any of us would care to admit in Gene Edwards' conclusion: "This era—the one I live in—

has proven to be unquestionably the most Bible-centered age since the days of the Pharisees; it also rivals their age for being the least Christ-centered. (And men today get just as mad as men of that former age when someone points out that fact.)"[12]

• And what of the weak sheep, those who can't seem to nuzzle their way into the hightech, fine-tuned programs of church professionals? What of the lamb that needs more than a 45-minute counseling appointment or a 25-minute exposition of the Word to understand how to walk with God? Whenever God measured the effectiveness of his shepherds in the Word, he always counted how effectively the weak were cared for, not how many of the strong muddied the pond. Too many people are falling through the cracks of the church's impersonalized structures.

A View from the Trenches

Sobering, isn't it? It's hard to believe that these vignettes sum up the same entity described in our first list of statistics. How do we know which to believe? Is the church beautifully clothed, or is she naked? It all depends on where we look.

On a grand, sweeping scale, enough statistics and stories can be garnered to set us at ease. If impressive architecture and elaborate programs fulfill our hunger, then we can sit back and have a cup of coffee. All is well.

If, however, our goals lie in Jesus Christ being glorifed in our world, where the needs of people are met even as they are being shaped after Jesus' image, then perhaps our coffee break is premature. To answer this cry we need to look more closely at our society, beneath statistics which can so easily gloss over personal pain. We need to look at people with names and faces, the very people we already know.

Take a look down your street: What do nonbelievers around you think of Jesus and his followers today? Do they hold them in respect or in contempt? Look down the pew: Why are people who are so faithful to the rituals of the church so empty and disheartened? Is Jesus a practical source of help for them?

Look into your own heart: Have you settled for a Christianity far beneath the one you read about in God's Word?

Walter Wangerin, a writer from Evansville, calls this "looking from the downside up." "I look from the downside up at the systems of the world: governmental systems, economic systems, class systems. From the topside down they look good, they comb their hair very well. From the downside up it doesn't look as good."[13] He found his vantage point in pastoring an inner-city church, and the view was painful. "I would rather not see from the downside up because I know many of the people who are participating in it. I like them. I don't want to be a prophet."

Who does? That's why we resist looking too closely, and instead turn away to comfortable generalities. Every pastor or evangelist caught in adultery, every money-grabbing appeal for funds, every person whose deep hurt goes unhealed, and every pretense of Christianity offends the God we profess to love—and should make us wince in embarrassment.

From the downside up you can see the pain and emptiness that infects our generation and the powerlessness of the church to fill it. Feel the horror of rejection which a young mother feels when her prayer request for a leukemia-stricken child is seemingly ignored as she listens to how God answered someone else's prayer to be a great football player or a Miss America. This is the view which the late David Watson must have seen when he concluded, "We live today in a sick church that desperately needs God's healing."[14]

Our dilemma is no better illustrated than in an encounter which Thomas Aquinas, a theologian of the thirteenth century, had with Pope Innocent IV. One day Aquinas found the Pope counting a large sum of money. "You see, Thomas," Pope Innocent said, "the church can no longer say, 'Silver and gold have I none' "—which is exactly what Peter and John, two of Christ's disciples, had said one morning when a lame beggar sought money from them. Instead, Peter and John healed the beggar's legs and sent him home dancing.

Aquinas thought about the Pope's statement for a moment and then replied, "True, holy Father, but neither can she now say, 'Rise up and walk.' "[15]

Though originally spoken as a lament for what Aquinas perceived as an unrecoverable past, these words could well serve as the epitaph of the Western church. It is far easier for us to handle money than to minister healing—so much so that many people doubt whether God even wants to heal today.

If you had to choose between a church that was poor but powerful and one that was rich but powerless, which would you prefer? Do you think God would choose any differently? But someone might object that one need not exclude the other. Perhaps inherently not, but it always seems to work out that way.

Today we are rich in the things of this world—money, political clout, even buildings that double as tourist attractions—but what appears to be our success may only testify to our failure. Colson points to how the gospel has been compromised in our push to make it popular: "Much of the Christianity we slickly market is nothing but a religious adaptation of the self-seeking values of secular culture."[16]

Such success is empty—only an illusion. "Even if the church seems to be succeeding, growth outruns depth and outward success masks inward emptiness."[17]

In the face of hurting people our success-by-numbers euphoria is woefully irrelevant. For those who have hoped for something better, I have great news: The heritage that Jesus bequeathed his church is more valuable than gold and silver, answering the deepest cries of our hurts and hungers!

True Riches

Nothing makes me hungrier for a dynamic Christianity than reading about the early church in the book of Acts. They weren't rich, perfect, or even culturally acceptable, but they exhibited a vitality of faith that stirs my heart. Four characteristics are particularly noteworthy.

1. They were preoccupied with Jesus. To the early church the resurrected Christ was not a mere theological fact. He who

had ascended before their very eyes had returned to be alive and present in his people, loving them, guiding them, and empowering them. Jesus himself said that his life in them by the Holy Spirit would be better than if he stayed with them (John 16:7), and the early church found it to be so.

He was the center of their message and the Lord of the church. They sought to hear his will and they obeyed it, not fleeing to the false safety of top-heavy institutions or name-brand celebrities. Christ's presence was real enough to take them through anything.

His presence should be no less real among us today, yet we lack a Christology of the present. Scholarship has wrangled over the preexistent Christ, the incarnate Christ, and the Christ of the second advent but is woefully deficient in a theology of the Christ of the present. For many he is only a distant voice of compassion even though he wants to be so much more.

When we lose that presence, spiritual death follows. George Whitefield was stirred by that loss in his generation early in the American colonies:

> I am persuaded [that] the generality of preachers talk of an unknown and unfelt Christ. The reason why congregations have been so dead is because they had dead men preaching to them.[18]

Remember how real God's presence was when you first surrendered to him? He only wanted it to get better from there!

2. *Their community had reality.* Unity and heartfelt love was the earmark of the early church. Even people who didn't accept their message marveled at how much they loved and cared for each other.

Every person, regardless of class or race or past lifestyle, found acceptance in the church. The rich and the poor, Jew and Gentile, slave and free served the Lord side-by-side. They never even contemplated homogeneous church ministry. Today we can't find a workable mission theology without it.

In their fellowship they did more than cut across cultural barriers—they sacrificed for each other's needs. They even sold land to buy food for others. Their love drew them to visit each other in jail even when doing so resulted in risk of their own arrest. Someone's weakness became an opportunity for someone else to serve, not judge or gossip. What a contrast to the backbiting and political infighting that characterize so much of what we call Christian fellowship today!

3. *Their ministry had power.* "My message and my preaching were not with wise and persuasive words," wrote the apostle Paul, "but with a demonstration of the Spirit's power, so that your faith might not rest on men's wisdom, but on God's power" (1 Corinthians 2:4,5).

Everything I have learned about ministry was geared to the art of persuasion through articulate and inspiring speech. I can weave a biblical argument around someone until he has no choice but to agree with me. Sadly, though, I've never seen it produce enduring change. Paul dissociated himself from such tactics, preferring to demonstrate how real the Spirit of God is, so that people trusted in God because they knew his reality.

Christianity to the first-century Christians was not primarily a confession of correct theology—it was God active in his creation to redeem people. The early church healed sick people, raised some from the dead, and liberated people captive to evil spirits.

Today we comfort the sick and bereaved and argue about the existence of demons. Yet God wants to share his power with us so that we can know how real he is and how practically he cares about us.

4. *They were willing to sacrifice.* The early Christians didn't follow Jesus to gain new cars and lakeview cabins. They followed him because he was Lord, enduring the violent reactions of a hostile culture. They were thrown to lions, boiled in oil, imprisoned, and stoned. Yet their faith only grew.

They faced conflicts resulting from their own desires but sought the will of God above personal gain. Their values were not in the material realm because they understood the abundant life not as temporal comfort but as living in the fullness of Jesus' presence.

Today many people are afraid to admit they are Christians for fear of being ridiculed. Rare is the believer who spends 15 minutes a day reading the Word and praying. Too often we soft-sell Christianity, pretending there's no cost because we're afraid we'll offend the Sunday-morning-only churchgoers. Sadly, too many people walk away from the church never having known a God worth sacrificing for.

All this is not to say that the early church didn't have problems. We know of occasions where evil men infiltrated the ranks of the church to exploit people for their own gain, where incest was tolerated, where believers lied to achieve status, and where communion was turned into a food fight. But we also see that these were the exception rather than the rule, and were dealt with openly and honestly. We know that believers were not perfect and that not everyone was healed of every sickness, but those who sought after God were increasingly changed into his likeness.

In comparison with this model I can only conclude that the church today is naked. What God has offered us is better than what we're living. We can know the same reality of the resurrected Jesus, the closeness of brotherly love, the power of supernatural ministry, and the joy far deeper than the lures of this life.

Not only did that first-century church touch this experience, but throughout church history there have been others who have captured a similar hunger for God, and with similar results. Though such people were not usually in the mainstream of church structure, God has continued to make his life available to his people. Even today reports from overseas tell us of believers finding this same reality. And if you look carefully you can find groups of believers hungering for such reality in America as well.

You can find it too. These characteristics we've examined all grew from the same root—from a depth of intimacy with God himself that is still possible today. The early church wasn't living up to a slate of expectations but was simply doing what came naturally to people who loved God with all their heart.

God wants us to experience that same vital Christianity. In the pages ahead I want to help you discover it.

3

The Emperor's New Clothes

You say, "I am rich; I have acquired wealth
and do not need a thing." But you do not realize
that you are wretched, pitiful, poor,
blind and naked.
—Revelation 3:17

What an amazing paradox—while we were stripped of the vitality of our relationship with God, we were handed enough statistics and programs to think ourselves successful!

Not only were we caught in a trap, but one so carefully constructed that we never recognized it as such even after it was sprung. Such a trick would be as difficult as convincing a naked man to walk down the street believing himself fully clothed.

Exactly!

And no one has illustrated this phenomenon better than Hans Christian Andersen in his tale *The Emperor's New Clothes*. The church today is more like this fictitious emperor than anyone would care to admit, and so are many of the people who fill its pews. How it happened to him illustrates how it happened to us.

The story is about an emperor who was more concerned about his appearance than about governing his people. Seizing that opportunity, two swindlers convinced him they could weave the most beautiful clothes ever made and also fashion them in such a way that they would be invisible to anyone who wasn't fit for his post or who was hopelessly stupid.

What could be better for the emperor? He could satiate his vanity and be a good ruler at the same time. He gave the self-proclaimed tailors money and the finest silk and gold thread. But the swindlers only pretended to make the clothes, pocketing the money and the material.

Fearing his own incompetence, the emperor sent his most honest aides to check on the progress of his clothing. The swindlers pretended to weave and sew, but the aides could see no clothes, for there weren't any. Thinking they would be thought unfit or stupid, they lavished praise on the nonexistent garments.

Eventually the emperor came to see the clothes. His aides were so enthused about them that he was sure of his own incompetence when he couldn't see them. So he joined the pretense, as did everyone who thought they alone weren't seeing the clothes. His aides suggested a parade to show the people his new clothes. Even though the emperor couldn't see them or even feel them, he pretended to put them on and went off to parade naked before the crowd.

Never had the emperor's clothes been such a success. Everyone praised their beauty—until a little child said, "But he hasn't got anything on!" The word quickly spread through the crowd as people realized they weren't the only ones not seeing the clothes. When the emperor overheard their shouts he realized his own nakedness, but he could only say, "I must go through with it now, procession and all."

The Power of Vested Interest

The point of this story is not vanity; it is vested interest. Though the ruse began with the emperor's pride, this alone could never have convinced him to walk down the street naked. The swindlers sprang the trap by giving everyone a good reason to believe what was not true.

But this is a fairy tale, you say; it doesn't happen in real life.

Anyone who has ever sat in a business meeting where personal interest rules the course will not only think it *can* happen but knows it *does* happen every day. Some of the strangest reasons can be used to defend the silliest project or idea as long as it is going to benefit someone. How fast a project goes through depends on how many people will profit from it. The swindlers made sure that everyone in town would be hurt if they didn't believe the lie. And we all know how easy it is to go with the crowd.

Well, maybe in business, but surely this can't happen in the church!

Not only can it, but it already has. This was exactly the problem Jesus addressed at the church in the Asian city of Laodicea: "You say, 'I am rich; I have acquired wealth and do not need a thing.' But you do not realize that you are wretched, pitiful, poor, blind and naked."

Church history is pocked with periods where the church was naked and didn't know it. It's easy for us now to look back at those generations, not sharing their vested interests, and see how believers sold out to political and personal corruption during the Middle Ages; to high finance prior to the Reformation; to terror and murder during the Inquisition; to naturalistic reason during the Enlightenment; and to liberalism early in this century. Those problems are so obvious to us now that we forget how articulately the church of those times was defended by well-intentioned people.

But this book is not concerned with past moments of nakedness—only with our own. Though our trade is different from the emperor's—he exchanged gold for air, and we exchange intimacy with God for gold itself and popularity with the world—the trap is still the same: We stay captive to deception by the same appeal to personal interest.

In the tale the first two officials to fall for the swindlers' deception were described as honest and capable. Yet for fear of losing status and position they pretended to see what their eyes told them was not there. Once the most honest fell for it, the others went along. The reality of the clothes became a secondary concern to protecting their image.

Anyone who does not gush with admiration for church institutions and activities today is accused of being arrogant or judgmental. That's our modern equivalent of being stupid or unfit. So, even though our Christian experience feels empty, we think we're the only ones to feel that way. To admit this is unthinkable, so we rationalize those nagging thoughts that tell us this can't really be what God had in mind. After all, there is always more to be gained by exploiting a system than there is by exposing it.

Today we are so impressed by our own efforts that through endless hours of talk shows and endless pages of fund-raising letters we congratulate ourselves: "Look how much we're doing for Jesus!" When we believe this thought, the trap is fully sprung. Our visions of a powerful and relevant church, with love enough for all and selfless sacrifice for God's kingdom, are filed away under the heading "Too Idealistic." We settle for the status quo as if it were all God intended—like a baby crocodile born in the zoo pond.

The emperor's nonexistent clothes were more successful than anything the emperor had ever worn. No real clothes would have gained such universal acceptance, because people's tastes differ too widely. Since nothing was there, each person made the pretense of seeing whatever he wanted to see. So it is with the church today; many people are making Christianity just what they want it to be, whatever best fits their interest. Widespread satisfaction with the church may only testify to its lack of substance.

The first person to be honest about the emperor's clothes was not all that courageous; he just didn't have any personal stake in the deception. He was too young to understand the necessity of denying reality to save face. It doesn't take great wisdom to unmask deceit—only a desire to look at things as they really are, not the way we want to see them.

But even when the truth was out, the emperor couldn't face it. He knew the people were right, but he had come too far now. He would really look like a fool if he had given half the realm's money for no clothes at all. What to do? What every self-respecting (there's the key) leader would do: stay the course, hoping by outward confidence to convince others that the clothes were really there and that the common people were stupid for not seeing them.

The church is naked. Who hasn't seen its deficiencies and wondered why we keep going on with it? But this is difficult to admit. If it is true, what do we do with our multimillion-dollar mortgages and operating expenses, our singing celebrities and their adoring fans, our committees and their policy statements?

So we go on, ever more ardently defending what is working so poorly. We risk becoming like the Pharisees to whom Jesus said, "You have no room for my word" (John 8:37). Their systems were set in concrete, providing a foundation for their own personal prestige. They would allow nothing to change that, not even truth.

Like the emperor, we conclude that it just might be better to make the best of a bad situation than to admit the mess we're in. But let us not be fooled: The world sees right through our empty confessions. Don't worry about them laughing at us for admitting it; they will only continue to laugh if we don't, and all the while blame God for what we are.

The Church at Laodicea

Since we too have fallen victim to the complacency of our imagined successes, it would be well for us to take a closer look at the church in Laodicea.

"You say, 'I am rich; I have acquired wealth and do not need a thing.'" Wealth marked this congregation, probably financially as well as with the influence in the community—two things that neither Jesus nor any of his disciples ever enjoyed. "But you do not realize that you are wretched, pitiful, poor, blind and naked." Their external wealth blinded them to the true status of their spiritual depth. What Jesus says to them in Revelation 3:14-22 applies to us no less.

> I know your deeds, that you are neither cold nor hot. I wish you were either one or the other! So, because you are lukewarm—neither hot nor cold—I am about to spit you out of my mouth (vv. 15,16).

This passage has made "lukewarm" the most feared accusation in Christendom even though we don't understand why a cold person is better than a lukewarm one. At least he's heating up, isn't he?

No, that misses the point entirely. A cold person is hard and rebellious. He makes no pretense of religion and offers it no lip service. Whether by indifference or outright hostility, a cold heart lives up to its confession: "There is no God, and even if there is, I'm going to do it my way."

A hot person is a zealot—one who burns with conviction. Like the cold person, he has no room for pretense or lip service. He doesn't merely talk about Jesus, go to church weekly, or watch Christian television. He seeks God wholeheartedly and obeys him even at great personal cost. Jesus must be first, and everything which distracts from that objective must go. Such people are uncomfortable to be around because their very lives expose our rationalizations for what they are—excuses to mix our Christianity with the attractions of the world.

In contrast to both of these, the lukewarm person's confession never matches his lifestyle. In fact his words are a substitute for his actions. He finds safety in pretense and lip service. The reason that Jesus would rather have us cold than lukewarm is because the lukewarm are no closer to him than the cold ones, but they don't even know it.

The lukewarm are those who redefine religion to fit themselves. To such people God cannot draw near. That's why Jesus chided the Pharisees for their pretense of religion almost in the same breath that he used to forgive the harlot. Being lukewarm allows people the dubious luxury of thinking they have the life of God yet still be free to pursue the objectives of this age. They can give God precedence with their mouth (saying the right thing is easy), their ceremonies (going the right places is habit-forming), and their actions (doing many right things keeps the conscience at bay), but they still don't have to surrender their will in everything.

The effect of their lukewarmness was measured in the impotence of their spirituality. Jesus pointed to three key areas that they were deficient in, and in doing so he gives us additional insight into their nakedness.

1. *Gold refined by fire.* Fire-refined gold is a common biblical analogy for an active faith that can stand the test of difficult circumstances. It is a far cry from the pseudofaith touted

today that attempts to compel God to give us anything we desire. Faith is not a gimmick; it is an intimate trust and dependence on God that is not hinged to circumstances but is grounded deep in God's nature.

Fire-refined faith takes us through the death of loved ones, unemployment, and persecution with a confidence that continues to trust God's love even when we cannot reconcile it with our circumstances. Such faith will find rest in God's presence and will give us wisdom to either help us bear the crises with God's strength or else show us how he wants to change those circumstances by his miraculous intervention.

2. *White clothes to wear.* The robes of righteousness are well-known in Scripture. Yet Christ said that they had none at Laodicea. Laodicea was not known for sin, but its righteousness was like that of the Pharisees—external, motivated only by the desire to increase spiritual status. Today the church can't even claim to *look* righteous, for promiscuity, greed, bitterness, and gossip abound. The list goes on and we try to excuse it by a bumper-sticker theology that says, "Be Patient God Isn't Finished With Me Yet!" or "Christians Aren't Perfect, Just Forgiven."

Shouldn't we be tired of falling victim to the same sins year after year, without seeing any hope of change? God wants us to wear his robes of righteousness, which spring up effortlessly from within people who are caught up in loving him. That's why true righteousness makes someone holy and not pious, humble and not prideful, compassionate and not disparaging. And though it is a lifelong process, every month we can see progress and find ourselves bearing God's image to people around us.

3. *Salve for your eyes.* Finally, the Laodiceans lacked discernment. Not only couldn't they see their own spiritual wretchedness, but they could see little else about God's working in their world. Discernment is the first thing to be covered by the crust of lukewarmness. The still, small voice diminishes and we learn to get along without it, living by principles and rules of conduct instead of the direction of the Holy Spirit.

A Call to Repentance

Though Jesus' letter to the Laodiceans is scathing, it also holds great promise. He gave them the opportunity to bury their nakedness in repentance and to buy back the spirituality they had squandered.

Did he literally mean they could cash in their wealth for faith, righteousness, and discernment? Of course not; we know these can't be bought with money. However, his choice of words was not arbitrary, for their pursuit of true wealth would cost them the false wealth they had gathered. If they were going to be honest they would have to risk their image to those who might be offended by a Christianity that offers challenge instead of mock comfort.

The same need and the same call to repentance await us. Our trappings look just as successful as those of the Laodiceans, and just as many lukewarm people fill our pews:

> The Church of Jesus Christ, now grown lukewarm and indifferent in pursuing its redemptive priestly ministry and corrective prophetic authority, largely has tolerated or participated in the dominant evils and errors of this sin-filled age.[1]

This statement was part of the *Manifesto for the Christian Church*, signed on July 4, 1986. It was produced by the Coalition on Revival, an organization whose steering committee includes such people as E.V. Hill, James Kennedy, Jay Kesler, Tim LaHaye, Harold Lindsell, and many others. The manifesto paints a bleak but accurate picture of the state of Western Christianity. Here are some other excerpts.

> We have built our own egos rather than advancing the kingdom of Christ.
> We have failed to confront falsehood and unrighteousness consistently in the Church or in the world because of our fear of man and of losing prestige or security.

We have been content to reduce the value of the transcendent gospel to mere creedal form, devoid of spiritual content or present reality by our harlotry with idols of personal peace and affluence.

We have heaped to ourselves teachers and pastors to tickle our ears with pleasant falsehoods and entertaining fables rather than convicting us of our sin and demanding that we live righteous lives of obedience to the Bible.

We have adopted the covetousness and materialism of our surrounding culture, seeking the approval of men and neglecting the fear of the Lord.

We will take a more specific look at some of these areas in future chapters as we see how naked they make us and what other options Jesus offers. The manifesto calls on the church to repent and recapture a vibrant faith firmly grounded in God's Word.

The opportunity to repent saves us from having to respond to our nakedness with condemnation. The same offer that Jesus made the Laodiceans still stands for us. We can return to him and recover what we have lost.

Our repentance, however, must be *personal*. Where does our life fall short? Do we want to live the way God has called us to? We must ask him to forgive us and restore to our life the faith, righteousness, and discernment he promised. Then we will rise again in this day to demonstrate the joy of devotion to Christ. We will wield his wisdom and power in our daily lives with such simplicity that others around us will know that the kingdom of God has come near them.

We will no longer be naked, but clothed in God's splendor!

4

Aren't You Hungry?

Blessed are those who hunger and thirst
for righteousness,
for they will be filled.
—Matthew 5:6

The most aggressive TV commercial I've ever seen was run by a fast-food hamburger chain a few years ago. Before my very eyes at five times normal size a hamburger sizzled above the licking flames. The background music, led by a driving drumbeat, grew louder. As it did the chant began, "Aren't you hunnnnnngry? Aren't you hunnnnnngry?" French fries suddenly splashed across the screen. Then the hamburger returned, this time on a toasted bun. The chant kept pounding. Soon I was on the edge of my seat, every saliva gland pumping at maximum capacity.

Then mercifully it was over—30 seconds that seemed like an eternity. Silence from the TV only highlighted my labored breathing. Of course I'm hungry; I'm always hungry. And I'm especially hungry in the middle of a fast, which seemed to be the only time I saw that commercial.

Hunger is a great driving force, and that commercial tapped it. We too must tap a different kind of hunger if we are going to pay the price to discard our nakedness.

Why Is Hunger So Important?

History demonstrates that reawakenings in the church come in cycles. Times of great spiritual fervor are followed by a gradual decline; then there is a fresh resurgence, and so on. As a result, many people have concluded that God's sovereignty is the impetus behind renewal. He earmarks certain periods for revival and others for dormancy.

Charles Finney found the same assumption in his day and attacked it with a vengeance. At the heart of every revival he studied he always found a person or group of people praying for that revival and expecting it—"on the watch-tower, constant in prayer till the blessing came."[1]

Revival is not the result of mere historical happenstance, and Finney knew that if people pinned all their hopes for change on God's sovereignty it would never come. God always wants to revive his people, but it is we who decide if he does. Recently I had breakfast with a well-published pastor who lamented how ineffective the church is today in making the gospel relevant for the unchurched. "Its structure is not conducive for it, and I do not see the church changing unless some worldwide catastrophe forces it to."

But we need not await such a catastrophe. Hunger for God's presence works just as well, for that is what grows out of catastrophes that spur revival. The following diagram of revival cycles will help explain why this is so. It is applicable to historical movements as well as to periods of renewal in our own lives.

The top of the chart marks those moments when God's presence is fresh, alive, and real; the bottom where God seems only a distant memory. The flow of events runs clockwise around the chart—three steps down the right side of the chart and three up the left.

Let's start at the top. I use the word "revival" to refer to the outpouring of God's grace, joy, and peace on his followers. Needs are met and his presence seems to fill every cranny of our lives. It is a time of excitement, when every day is an adventure to see what God wants to do next around us. Bondages are healed, deception is dispelled, character is developed in times of affliction, and love and humility abound in relationships with other people.

The first step away from revival is complacency. Everything has been so wonderful and effortless that we stop pressing on and instead become caretakers of the status quo. Our hunger for God is dulled. We don't need him as much for our own

needs, and we lose his vision of extending the life of his kingdom to a dying world. But God's life is like a river: The moment it stops flowing it begins to stagnate.

As our perception of his presence wanes, we compensate by falling in love with God's gifts, eventually loving them more than we love him and using them for our own gain. God describes that process with Israel in Ezekiel 16. He describes Israel as an abandoned child, lying naked in a field, covered with blood. God finds her, takes her home, cleans her up, clothes her in beautiful clothes, and teaches her how to be a lady. What a marvelous story—until the young lady falls in love with her own beauty. She begins to use her beauty to get what she wants from others, and turns to prostitution.

She forgot the God who rescued her. The final step toward spiritual death is rarely active rebellion; it is neglect. Israel was rebuked for this trap over and over again. Enemies or drought rose up against them, and they fell on their faces to pray and repent. God then routed the enemy or blessed his people with rain. When prosperity returned they went off to enjoy it.

How often I've seen that happen! People caught in trouble turn to God for help when they need a job or a marriage put back together. Their newfound relationship with God begins to change them and their circumstances, and the trouble is soon resolved. As time passes they don't seek God as aggressively as at the start. Their job or marriage subtly become more important than God.

When God is forgotten, or takes second chair to our enjoyment of his blessings, spiritual life quickly dries up. Prayers seem only to bounce off the walls, and the Word seems dry. All the forms and vocabulary still persist, but they are lifeless without God's presence. In fact religious activity often increases during this time in an attempt to compensate for the emptiness.

During these times God's nature is sorely misunderstood. When people cry out in need but find that their prayers aren't answered, they get angry with God, for he doesn't seem to live up to his own theology. Jeremiah addressed this need in his own generation:

> They have turned their backs to me and not their faces; yet when they are in trouble they say, "Come and save us!" Where then are the gods you made for yourselves? Let them come if they can save you when you are in trouble! (Jeremiah 2:27,28).

How can we expect God to jump to our attention in the things we pray about when we've not been listening to him, to his concerns? Unanswered prayers that seem to obviously be in God's will are a sure indication that we've come to the bottom of the cycle.

Unfortunately, at times like this people are often encouraged to just hang in there: "Everyone goes through dry times; it will pass." Don't believe it, and don't acclimate yourself to God's inactivity. Remember what it was like when God was moving in your life, and let yourself get hungry to be there again.

Hunger is your first step back up the chart. In the face of God's promises all that the world offers really is empty. Hunger will cause you to seek the Lord wholeheartedly, putting him above everything else. Heartfelt prayer and repentance will break the crust of complacency, opening you once again to his presence. Transformation follows, and with it the joy and excitement of revival.

Notice the pivotal moments in this chart: complacency and hunger. Complacency starts us on the road to deadness, taking our eyes off God and putting them on the cares of this world. Conversely, hunger puts our hearts back on God, making us willing to pay whatever cost is necessary to know God in his fullness. That's why Jesus said, "The kingdom of heaven has been forcefully advancing, and forceful men lay hold of it" (Matthew 11:12).

God did not create us to spin around this cycle from high to low. Our challenge as believers is to *get* hungry and *stay* hungry for God.

"Here, Kitty, Kitty!"

Mama Cat was the mice exterminator on the grape ranch where I grew up in central California. She had a name, but we never used it. At three litters of kittens per year, with rarely less than eight kittens per litter, no other name would do. We looked forward to each new batch and to playing with the young kittens.

Then we got Penney, a German shepherd pup who was attacked her first day home by Mama Cat for wandering too near her most recent brood. Penney's snout was bloodied by a few well-placed claws. Needless to say, they weren't good friends after that, and when Penney finally grew up, Mama Cat moved her deliveries elsewhere.

Now we would only see her new offspring when she brought them up to the house, ready to wean them. They would move into a thick hedge outside our back door where the dog could not get them. Having had no human contact for two to three months, the kittens were terrified of us. If we even got close they would hiss and spit, lashing out with their claws. "You either have to tame those cats so we can give them away or else I'll have to dispose of them." My dad's words sounded harsh, but we knew there was no other option.

How do you tame wild cats? We used their hunger. We began by putting a bowl of warm milk inside the hedge. When they started drinking it, Mama Cat would wean them. Now they needed us, and we would put the bowl just outside the hedge and stay to watch them. They hated to eat with us present there, but their hunger forced them to come anyway. In ensuing days we shortened the distance between us and the bowl until we were close enough to pet them while they ate. Finally they would come when we called them, milk or no milk; they were our friends at last.

All this because of hunger! All they wanted was dinner, but we know that food alone wouldn't save them. They needed to be tamed, and hunger was a motive strong enough to make the larger change they needed. Our flesh is just like those little kittens—hostile to God. Everything in this world and in our old nature pulls us away from his kingdom. The only thing that will take us through the process of reconciliation is hunger for God that keeps driving us to him in good times and bad. But such hunger is a rare commodity in this age.

Hunger in an Age of Defensiveness

Like everyone in Hans Christian Andersen's tale, we find it threatening to challenge the status quo. It may not be what we want, but at least there's no more risk in it. We learn to get by and don't want anyone upsetting the balance.

The Pharisees had the same problem. John the Baptist and Jesus were enigmas to them. They noted a dynamic in their ministries that they sorely lacked, but they could never bring themselves to admit it. Instead they quibbled over theology ("Should we pay taxes?") and methodology ("Stop healing on the Sabbath."). In one encounter they asked Jesus directly, "By what authority are you doing these things?" (Matthew 21:23-27).

Jesus' response seemed to dodge the issue. Instead of answering their question, Jesus forced them into withdrawing it: "I will also ask you one question. If you answer me, I will tell you by what authority I am doing these things. John's baptism—where did it come from?"

The Pharisees huddled. "If we say, 'From heaven,' he will ask, 'Then why don't you believe him?' But if we say, 'From men'—we are afraid of the people, for they all hold that John was a prophet." They finally answered, "We don't know."

Jesus proved his point. The only reason they couldn't understand his ministry is because they didn't want to. They refused to listen to anything that challenged their vested interest, preferring the false power of ignorance to the vulnerability of hunger.

Don't we do the same? A young man sat in my office years ago and shared with me his desire to walk in a gospel more filled with power than he saw in the church around him. "I'm going to start seeking God one hour every day and find out how I can live like the early church lived."

My first thought was to discourage him. I didn't have an hour to spend every day right now, and if he did he might have a more powerful walk than I was modeling. I was threatened, and to my shame I discouraged his hunger: "Don't you think if God wanted to do more in his church he'd be showing that to leaders today?"

This same thing happened when the charismatic renewal began in the 60's. Suddenly people were talking about a God who wanted to be active, talking to his people and performing miracles. I know people who found that threatening. They had walked with God for 40 years and had never seen him do any kind of miracle.

Their line of reasoning ran like this: "If God wants to do these things today, why haven't I heard about it before now? Since I've been faithful to him, he certainly wouldn't leave me out. Therefore God's miracles can't be for today." They may even have prayed for God's special work in desperate moments of the past, only to see their prayers go unanswered. But instead of acknowledging this forthrightly, they cloaked their disagreements in theological terms and pointed to excess and abuse within the movement to discount it. The very thing that God was doing to include them they used as a basis to resist him.

Our culture does that to us. In an age of defensiveness, hunger is unthinkable. We consider successful those who are self-assured, confident, and fulfilled; so even if we're not any of these, we must pretend to be. We have come to possess the fragile identities on which our culture is so fixated; we are unable to admit need, unmet dreams, or mistakes. Too many of our relationships are based on having to project a flawless performance; gaining acceptance forces us to justify everything we do.

In such a climate, hungry people are regarded at best as fanatics and at worst as rebels. "Sensible" people accept the status quo for what it is and use it as advantageously as possible. Like the Pharisees, we hunger more to preserve our place in the eyes of those around us than to admit our need to change. That may not be what we want to do, but it's what we do by default.

In Matthew 11:2,3 John asked a question very similar to that of the Pharisees. He got his answer because even though he had significant vested interest in Jesus, he wanted the truth. John had validated Jesus' ministry, sending his own disciples to serve him. If Jesus weren't the Messiah, John would have to face up to the fact that he had failed in his mission to be a forerunner for the Christ. Risk it he did, though, because he wanted to *be* right more than he wanted to *appear* right.

How Do We Create Hunger?

All the great people of God throughout history were stirred both by a vision that burned in their hearts and by their ability to look at the status quo and admit that it did not live up to their vision. That dichotomy alone creates hunger—to see what can be and to admit that it isn't here yet. Our obedience is all that is needed to bridge the two. This is what produces the Luthers, the Wesleys, the Bonhoeffers. They saw a great disparity in their day between biblical promise and cultural reality, and they set about to narrow the gap.

If we're going to be hungry for God in this age, we too need to take two looks. The first is a joyful one: Look at the promises in God's Word for people who walk with him. Our model is Jesus' ministry with his disciples and the early church in Acts.

We need to dream of God's kingdom among us, making his loving presence real in the harshness of our world. We need to see believers who love God enough to suffer for him, people bound by demonic darkness exploding into the freedom of God's life, a formerly lame man dancing in joy, a harlot fully forgiven. We need to see prayers consistently answered, darkness-bound people finding freedom in Christ, believers relinquishing their lives in the face of death.

Promises greater than our present experience await us. Jesus said that when we really see the beauty of God's kingdom, we will stop at nothing to apprehend it. It is a pearl of great price and at its heart is an intimate relationship with the Lord of glory. Imagine the splendor of God's love holding us, his voice guiding us, his power sustaining us every day.

The other look we need to take is not so glorious, but nonetheless necessary. God's promises must be superimposed over our own experience to show us where we fall short. Promise alone is not enough, since we have a tendency to conform God's promises to our present circumstances instead of hungering for change. Hunger can only flourish when we recognize that our present circumstances don't measure up to God's promise.

Charles Finney said, "A revival always includes conviction of sin on the part of the church."[2] That's what the Old Testament prophets did to try to shake their generations out of complacency. This is a difficult look to take, and one often ignored in preference to hearing about self-esteem, peace of mind, and financial prosperity. Editors know that people won't pay good money for bad news. They'll only do that at the doctor and dentist, because we can't hide physical disease as cleverly as we can spiritual. Jeremiah faced the same problem:

> The prophets prophesy lies, the priests rule by their own authority, and my people love it this way. But what will you do in the end? (Jeremiah 5:31).

God has continually sent prophets to strip the facade off religion and to force people to look squarely at the state of their spiritual life. That's why prophets are only honored after they die. Isaiah, Jeremiah, and Elijah were hated by nearly everyone in their day. Jesus even noted this fact to the Pharisees: "Woe to you, because you build tombs for the prophets, and it was your forefathers who killed them" (Luke 11:47).

Are we any different today? Could Luther and Wesley speak in our pulpits? As long as their words apply to another generation, we revere them. Would we tolerate them if they spoke the same about things we hold dear? Let's try it!

Luther spoke out passionately against Rome's practice of selling indulgences—offering spiritual forgiveness and status for money that was put into a building fund at the Vatican. Here's what he said:

> The revenues of all Christendom are being sucked into this insatiable basilica. The Germans laugh at calling this the common treasure of Christendom. Before long all the churches, palaces, walls and bridges of Rome will be built out of our money. First of all, we should rear living temples, not local churches. . . . He—the pope—would do better to sell St. Peter's and give the money to the poor folk who are being fleeced by the hawkers of indulgences.[3]

Of course we know the Roman Church of that day had its abuses—even the Catholic Church today admits that fact. What if Martin Luther were alive today? Do you think he would look on our fund-raising techniques today with any less disgust? Do you think he would see any difference between the Pope's indulgences and the PTL Network's fund-raising plan of selling a place in a "Hall of Faith" to anyone who sent them a thousand dollars? It's still spiritual status to the highest bidder. Would we listen to Luther's words if he were to apply them to someone living today?

> The revenues of all Christendom are being sucked into this insatiable TV ministry. The world laughs at calling

this the common treasure of Christendom. Before long all the buildings of Heritage Village will be built out of our money. First of all we should rear living temples, not TV stations. He—Jim Bakker—would do better to sell Heritage Village and give the money to the poor folk who are being fleeced by the hawkers of "Hall of Faith" plaques.

Doesn't sound too good, does it? We would accuse Luther of having a lack of love, since after all Aunt Josie gave her heart to Jesus by watching that show. We forget that the prophets were talking about real people and risked offending their own generations to challenge them to the heights of God's glory.

The abuses of Christianity today are many. The example above isn't the only one, just one of the most blatant. Yet who is crying out against the abuses of our day? We think Christian unity and charity demands that we close our eyes to whatever attempts to pass itself off as the work of God. But when such a work ceases to bear any resemblance to the genuine article, someone had better speak out, even if he is labeled a rebel, for these abuses do far more to rob people of intimacy with God than anything the world could ever do. Sheldon Vanauken is right: "It isn't the enemy lurking outside the cathedral door that the church needs to fear, but the enemy within."[4]

Jesus warned his disciples on two occasions (John 16:1-4 and Luke 12:11,12) that true disciples would often be at odds with the religious system of the day. In every age the church is called to take the narrow road away from the acclamation and influence of those who would use the church for their own ends. Its most dangerous days have been when the visible church, infatuated with itself, has fought against people who hunger for God.

The remainder of this book is written in chapter couplets. In the first chapter of each couplet we will push contemporary Christianity to the mirror of God's Word. Such a juxtaposition is rarely pretty, but we must see not only *that* we are naked, but *why* we are. What does a lifeless Christianity offer our flesh so that it entices us away from intimacy with God?

Are you hungry enough to take such a look honestly? The lack of spiritual hunger is killing us. Os Guiness, author of *The Gravedigger Files*, had this to say about selecting that unusual title: "Christianity contributed significantly to the rise of the modern world, it has committed itself uncritically to the world it helped create and it has been undermined by its own efforts. The church, therefore, is becoming its own gravedigger."[5]

The second chapter of each couplet will be a blueprint for you to build your own intimate walk with God. This book is less about institutional change than personal change. Its mission will only be fulfilled as it brings you into a deeper relationship with the Father through Jesus Christ.

Can It Happen for Me?

Seeing a distant vision and seeing how far short of it we fall is not enough to create hunger unless we know how to make that vision our own experience. My hunger for that sizzling hamburger in the commercial is only a good thing if I have the freedom or money to buy one. On the days I was fasting, the food only frustrated me. Should we peer at God's life as a distant, unattainable promise? No, the reality of God's life is within the reach of us all.

We were created to be a people of God's presence, not of mere theology or ethics. We can know the living God and know what it means to have him live his life through us. It's a process where each step is full of more glory and wonder than the last. Surprises abound as God reveals himself to us and we are changed according to his image.

That makes me hungry. How about you? I can offer you nothing more valuable in these pages than the gift of hunger.

Discovering God's Presence

5

Of Course I Love God!

These people come near to me
with their mouth and honor me
with their lips, but their hearts
are far from me.
—Isaiah 29:13

"You have to help me!" The look in her eyes confirmed the desperation in her voice.

She had called me 20 minutes before on a friend's recommendation, needing to see a pastor. She was barely 20, a willowy brunette. "The man I've been living with moved out on me a month ago. To get back at him I'm having an affair with his best friend."

"What can I do for you?" I asked, trying to feel out the situation.

Tears began to flow. "I'm so torn up inside. I can't sleep at night. I've got to find some peace."

Amazing! She didn't seem ashamed of her immorality or vengeance. "Why did you come to see me?"

"I'm a Christian," she said, looking shocked that I had asked. (I'm sure I looked as shocked at her answer.)

"What do you mean you're a Christian?"

"I love God, you know. Even went forward a couple of years ago to be born again. I believe he died on the cross and all that."

I couldn't believe my ears. "You see no conflict between your confession of Christianity and the lifestyle you're living?"

"Should I?" Her shocked look returned.

I'll spare you her excuses, but I helped her see the disparity between the Christianity she professed and the life she was living. I offered her healing in Jesus from her hurts, but she

47

didn't want to give up her life, and in the end she decided she would find her peace another way.

Regrettably, she is not an isolated case. For too many people Christianity is only a creed to confess or ritual to follow. Its impact is only mental, far removed from the realities of everyday living. Such Christianity is full of form but devoid of substance, and God never intended it to be that way.

Abstracting Reality

A.W. Tozer saw how little Christianity was built around the practical presence of God:

> If the Holy Spirit was withdrawn from the church today, 95% of what we do would go on and no one would know the difference. If the Holy Spirit had been withdrawn from the New Testament church 95% of what they did would stop and everybody would know the difference.[1]

Today God is an abstraction, existing in an unseen and unfelt spiritual realm. People can only please him by following his rules—going to church, tithing, and being good to their neighbor. But God wants to be so much more real than that. He wants to be closer to us than our best friend and to participate in our daily lives.

Walter Wangerin defines abstraction as "the removing of God from experiential life."[2] Some people do it out of ignorance, never having heard how practical God's presence was meant to be. Their theology might be right, but they've never understood the implications of their beliefs. Wangerin continues:

> It is not hard to argue the immanence of God. Why, it is one of our doctrines. . . . There's the sticking point. So long as it remains a doctrine alone, a truth to be taught, immanence continues an abstraction and he is not immanent.[3]

But even to those of us who do understand how closely God wants to be involved in our lives, abstraction is a trap that can catch us again and again. Israel fell into this trap often. During one of those times God gave Isaiah a strong rebuke for them, in effect saying, "I no longer participate in your rituals, and no one missed me." To help us understand how challenging his words were to them, and how applicable they are to us, let me substitute in this passage some of our forms of worship for theirs:

> The multitude of your tithes and offerings—what are they to me? I have more than enough of your good works, evangelistic crusades, and missionary teas. I have no pleasure in your uplifted hands or your singing in tongues. When you come to meet with me who has asked this of you, this trampling of my courts?
>
> Stop bringing meaningless offerings! Your services are detestable to me. Sunday mornings, Wednesday nights, and your retreats, I cannot bear your evil assemblies. Your Christmas pageants and Easter festivals my soul hates. They have become a burden to me. I am weary of bearing them. When you spread out your hands in prayer, I will hide my eyes from you (Isaiah 1:11-15).

Even though Israel's forms of worship were ones that God had mandated for them, he was angry because their hearts were no longer in them. Long after they had turned from obeying him to seeking their own pleasure, they had continued the guise of worship.

How easily religious forms outlive the reality that spawned them! We continue the motions, but God is no longer the object of our pursuit. When that happens our actions become lifeless traditions and can easily become more sacred than God himself. David Duplessis saw this danger: "Every church has its traditions, and they would rather sacrifice the truth of Scripture than sacrifice their tradition."[4]

Obviously this is abstraction at its worst, but its impact is felt in so many more subtle ways. It allows us to push God out of our lives without admitting to it, because his name and activities still fill so much of our time.

Nowhere is this seen more pointedly than in the popular definition of *agape* love. Many are teaching that God's agape love is a love that transcends feelings. It is based on a commitment to do what's right even if one has no personal feelings for the object of that action. We are even told that agape love is what Jesus demonstrated on the cross. What a weakened view of God's love!

God loves you with affection that runs deeper than any human could possibly have for you. The cross was not a token—a dying commitment to people he was supposed to save. The cross was love—full, rich, and emotional. He saw us in the anguish of our sin, and because he had compassion for us he took our sin to the cross that we might be free of it. We see Jesus' agape love when he wept over Jerusalem's rejection, when he touched a leper with healing, and when he let a prostitute pour perfume on his feet.

He loves you the same way. He's not just committed to you. He wanted you before you ever knew he existed. When he fills our heart his Spirit in us cries out with the extremely personal "Abba Father"—"Daddy." God's love to us is that personal and that real. It overwhelms us with the magnificence of his goodness. Some may mock that as sloppy agape, but that is the love God wants to heap upon you.

And that's the love he wants us to have for others—deep affection for other believers and compassion for the world. Commitment is a cheap substitute by comparison and is only the last gasp of a generation dying in abstraction. Because feelings supposedly don't count, we can with all piety say we love some people even though we can't stand them and our stomach lurches every time they walk into a room.

This kind of thinking produces a false spirituality that insulates us from God's work in our lives. One morning a few years ago a young woman from the church phoned me just to tell me what a lousy pastor I was, and she did so with a vengeance. She had misunderstood a conversation I had with her husband. Her accusations, based on secondhand information, were far from accurate. She was hurt and angry and in my mind unjustifiably so.

Explaining that to her, however, proved to be impossible. She reacted with such harshness that I knew the only chance for healing lay in confession rather than eloquent defense. I weighed my choices: apologize for the misunderstanding or defend my actions. "I'm sorry you're hurt," I finally said; "will you forgive me?"

"Oh, Wayne, I already have," was her reply, and she said it so piously I almost slammed the phone down in anger. I was speechless. If I had already been forgiven, what were these verbal lashings for, recreation?

Obviously she had not forgiven me. What disturbed me most was that she genuinely thought she had. That's what happens when Christianity becomes an abstraction. It deceives us into hypocrisy and keeps us from letting God heal relationships, filling them with his warmth and affection.

Christianity removed from human experience ceases to be Christianity at all. Abstraction trades the real work of God in our lives for words and rituals. The effects are devastating, leaving us with a Christianity that only exists in the mind, not the heart.

No longer do we look for God's leading. Instead we pray, plan, and hold services, only assuming that God will bless them. While reading a professional journal for church leadership I came across an article about making decisions in the church. Four ways were given by a college professor: voting, appointing an expert, statistical averaging, and consensus.[5] Not one of them told how a group of people could hear the voice of the Lord together and move in confidence. We have followed Israel into the sin of assumption: "Their priests did not ask, 'Where is the Lord?' " (Jeremiah 2:8).

Don't we do the same thing by launching into our day with a prayer that Jesus will bless what we're going to do? Don't we believe he has anything more to say to us than our own minds can reason out? Abstraction reduces spiritual growth from following God to mere observance of law, or, as we call them today, "principles." But God wants to be as close to you as your own breath, with the reality of his presence guiding you and transforming you by his love.

Nothing turns off the next generation quicker than believers whose words don't match their experience. Children and new converts easily see where we deceive ourselves, just like the little boy in *The Emperor's New Clothes*. They will not tolerate form without substance, and many of them reject Christianity because they see nothing real about it.

The Great Divorce

Much of Christianity today divorces the truth of the gospel from the reality of daily living. Even though this results in a lifeless Christianity, sometimes that is easier to endure than facing reality.

1. *Reality won't let us substitute religious tradition for personal sacrifice.* Religious routine is the first thing we grab when the freshness of God's presence dries up—and who hasn't experienced such dry times? One day our relationship with God is fresh and alive, and then suddenly our prayers and Bible reading turn empty; even going to church is a chore.

We have two options here: We can just learn to be content with rituals, trying to make the best of them, or else we can throw ourselves before God to find out why things have dried up and how we can change to keep moving ahead. Isn't the first option infinitely better?

Answered prayer is a good example of this. If God doesn't move in response to our prayers, we have a number of ready-made reasons why this shouldn't bother us.

- God doesn't answer prayers today; that was only for the apostles.
- We just have to trust God's sovereignty. One can only hope for the best.

- God knows that not answering this prayer will make me a better person.
- God doesn't answer selfish prayers, so my prayer must have been selfish.

Abstraction creates a Christianity that can run without God's involvement. If he answers, fine; if not, we can go on without him. Reality, on the other hand, forces us to seek God's face with greater fervor. But this risks finding out what God wants to change in us, and something in all of us would rather slip into the comfort of religious ritual than risk the personal sacrifice which God might ask of us.

2. *Reality demands effectiveness.* If we are going to say that salvation in Christ offers people a personal relationship with God, then we had better see them through to it, since this doesn't just automatically happen. I've known many people who have gone forward to receive Christ and yet continue under a deep weight of guilt, or who acknowledge that they don't feel like they're really experiencing the fullness of Jesus' presence. Abstraction tells them to just press ahead, accepting their new relationship "by faith."

Reality cannot accept that misapplication of theology. How can the King of Glory ride into someone's heart unnoticed? When I meet someone like that I usually assume that Jesus hasn't entered his heart—yet!

I faced this very thing with a young man I met after a midweek service many years ago. He had been prayed for many times to receive Christ, but he still carried a deep guilt that paralyzed him from growing in Christ. I tried to encourage him with 1 John 1:9 and some other Scriptures to help him accept the forgiveness I was sure he must have had. But he persisted. He had tried that before and it hadn't worked.

We agreed to meet the next day to explore his problem more deeply. Eventually I discovered that he had major reservations about serving God. He enjoyed his life in sin, and only wanted to be saved to escape eternal punishment for his sin. No wonder he didn't feel forgiven—he wasn't! In the end he decided to fully submit to Christ, and then he knew the full release of forgiveness of sin. "I really feel clean!" he beamed.

It's not easy to confront someone who is feeling unforgiven, but when you take ministry out of the abstract you have no choice. Platitudes do not suffice. In ministry the outward responses of A + B + C don't always equal D. Often there are unseen ingredients that need to be searched out carefully.

3. *Reality won't let us substitute saying for doing.* Years ago I read about a university study that measured the difference between what people *say* they will do and what they will actually do. A random sample was split into two groups. The first was notified that they were being polled to measure community spirit in America. They were asked to donate three hours of their time on Saturday to help collect money in their neighborhood to fight cancer. The second group was not told they were being polled, but they were asked to give three hours of their next Saturday to help collect for a fund drive.

Something like 73 percent said they would be willing if asked, but only about 5 percent of those asked to do it said they would—an astounding difference. Anyone who has worked with volunteers knows how accurate this statistic is. We've confused confessing with *being* and willing with *doing*. Saying "I forgive" is easier than actually forgiving. Going forward is not the same as giving your life to God.

Looking back at the Scripture from Isaiah, we can see that Israel sought to establish God's presence by their sacrifice. He said to do it, and they were doing it, so he must be present with them. There's no more validity in that reasoning than to say that just because we put lots of believers in the same room and sing songs to God he is there to participate.

I'm convinced that someone who really understands the way of the cross will find legalism to be an easy course by comparison. It is one thing to read the Word ten minutes a day and quite another to actually feed on it. The former is automatic and takes nothing more than ten minutes of the day while the latter demands attention, concentration, and openness to the Spirit.

4. *Reality is often painful.* It's amazing to me how many people who really believe that a personal relationship with Jesus is essential to salvation fudge on that matter when a close relative or friend dies. "After all, they were sincere in their own way and went to church when they could." In many ways reality faces us with difficult implications we would rather avoid.

Back to Reality

I am always challenged by people who are ready to abandon abstraction for a vital Christian experience. Richard Foster records for us such a personal moment over unanswered prayer: "I determined to learn to pray so that my experience conformed to the words of Jesus rather than trying to make His words conform to my impoverished experience."[6]

What a risky but powerful pursuit! Moses was adamant about it: "If your Presence does not go with us, do not send us up from here" (Exodus 33:15). He wasn't going to proceed with any religious charade if God wasn't in it.

Jesus was adamant too. The Pharisees claimed to be children of Abraham, with all the status they thought this deserved. Even though they talked of righteousness, tithing, and God's mercy, Jesus didn't indulge their pretense: "You belong to your father, the devil" (John 8:44). Their self-imposed deception had to end, not only for their own good but also to end the bad reputation God was getting at their hand.

And so do we deceive ourselves when we persist with religious traditions that have long lost their life. Christianity does not exist in words and rituals unless it first thrives in the heart. Moving back from abstraction to honesty can be difficult, but the rewards far outweigh any cost involved.

Elijah was one of Israel's most powerful prophets, and he wasn't afraid to be honest. Yet in 1 Kings 19 we find him hiding in fear of Jezebel. "I've had enough," he laments to God. "Take my life; I am no better than my ancestors." He tells God how much he has labored for him, and that he is the only faithful one left.

Elijah is fortunate that he didn't come to me for counseling a few years ago! I know how hard I would have tried to get his mind off his feelings: "You can't run on feelings, you know. God is always with us no matter how bad it looks. Just trust him and everything will work out okay." In doing so I would have robbed Elijah of perhaps the most powerful moment of his life. God instructed him to go to Mount Horeb and stand on the edge of a mountain as he watched a mighty wind and a devastating earthquake. Then in a gentle whisper God came and Elijah stood before him.

Elijah knew he needed the presence of God, and he found it. The same opportunity is yours. Come, feast of God's presence. You'll find that he wants to be a practical part of your life, and that reality is nothing to fear at all.

6

Real Salvation

*Believe in the Lord Jesus,
and you will be saved.*
—Acts 16:31

The pastor could hardly contain himself as he told me about his church's door-to-door evangelism program: "In the last five months we've had over 175 people give their lives to Jesus!"

I was there to do some guest speaking, and I knew that only about 50 people were attending the church. "Where are they?" I asked.

"Come on, Wayne, you know as well as I do that less than 1 percent ever make their faith active."

He was right—I did know that. Even the largest and most expensive evangelism campaigns don't do much better. I always wonder why we get so excited about such efforts. Don't get me wrong—I'm grateful that at least a handful of people want to take time on a Saturday to share their faith. I'm excited about the two people (a generous 1 percent) who found a new life with Christ. But my joy is mitigated when I think about the other 173.

Did they go through the motions of accepting Jesus just to get the visitors off their doorstep? How silly we must look when we're deceived so easily!

Did they think a sinner's prayer alone completes the Christian experience? If so, I'm afraid we've deceived them at the same time we've disarmed the conviction of the Holy Spirit that might well have brought them to Christ.

Did they genuinely want to walk with Jesus, but no one showed them how? Then we're only leaving a wake of frustrated people whose form of Christianity won't fulfill its promise.

The reason why so many people don't know God as a present, personal reality begins with conversion itself. When people make the "right" responses we record their statistic without ever ensuring that they have really opened themselves to God and know how to walk on in him.

What does it really mean to be a Christian? The ramifications of that question run to the heart of the church's nakedness both on the doorsteps of our witnessing programs and in the pews of our sanctuaries.

Evangelists thunder about the moment at judgment day when your neighbor on his way to hell looks at you and cries out, "Why didn't you tell me?" To be honest, I'm also concerned about the person sitting two pews in front of me. He may have opened his heart to God at one point, but he no longer holds an active faith because he is either unconcerned or unaware that life with God is more than sitting in a pew.

Christianity Made Easy

Admittedly the topic of conversion is a tricky one, particularly if we're only preoccupied with whether a person qualifies for heaven or not. Wanting to include as many as possible, we have the tendency to build a wider road than Jesus did.

Ann Landers, writing to a Christian mother concerned about her son's impending marriage to a Jewish girl, seems to think a good life will suffice: "Try to view the situation from a broader point of view. It is this: Eternal life is granted to all people who live according to God's laws."[1] I'm all for mothers accepting future daughters-in-law, but do we have to change God's covenant to do it? Scripture clearly states that we'll never merit salvation by our own good works: "For if righteousness could be gained through the law, Christ died for nothing!" (Galatians 2:21).

Peter Wagner, a leader in the church growth movement, describes his concept of active church members: "They may not be there every Sunday, but they attend at least occasionally, they make some financial contribution to the church, they regard the church as 'my church,' they expect that their young children will also become members, and they look at the church for rites of passage such as weddings and funerals."[2] I know that church-growth people need something to count, but what has any of this to do with whether someone is loving God and serving him wholeheartedly?

Perhaps the most popular determination today is whether someone has said the sinner's prayer. Many feel that it encapsulates all the responses asked of us for salvation—confession of sin and surrender to Jesus' lordship. And for the most part it does, except that using it alone reduces salvation to an outward act that may not express the desire of the heart. To that extent the sinner's prayer can become nothing more than the New Testament equivalent of Old Testament circumcision.

God told Abraham that at eight days old every male was to be circumcised as a sign of his covenant with Israel. Eventually the rite became more important than the objective for which it was given. Even in those periods when Israel was disobedient to God, every male child was still being circumcised. But the act itself, without the heart surrendering to God, was meaningless.

The same is true of our "sinner's prayer." Many have gone through the ritual, thinking it a small price to pay to escape guilt or hell. In our haste to bring people into God's kingdom we too have lost true purpose to the outward form. We count converts by sinner's prayers or baptisms, never questioning whether these people are finding communion with God.

The result, as observed by one writer, is that even though many people are professing to be born again, it's not making much difference.

> One of the distressing aspects of the "born again" boom is that it makes so little impact on Christian society. Crime is up. Marriages are breaking down at an ever-increasing rate. Secularism is growing. Yet, with each passing day, more and more people profess to be born again.[3]

It is obvious that something is wrong. Many people are calling themselves "Christian" who do not have the lifestyle to back it up. Our attempts to include everyone have helped no one, and as a result our churches are full of six different varieties of pseudo-Christians.

• *Pretend Christians* only go through the motions of religion for the benefits of being thought a Christian. It might please a spouse, help them make business contacts, or give their children a religious heritage, but they are not interested in growing closer to God or obeying his will.

• *Cultural Christians* think they inherit Christianity from previous generations. These people love chaplains in legislatures, "Now-I-lay-me-down-to-sleep" prayers, and invocations at graduations. Cultural Christians produce the kind of headlines we see coming out of Ireland: "Catholics Kill Four More Protestants In Belfast."

God gets more bad press from Pretend and Cultural Christians than from any other variety. They are hypocrites of the worst order, exploiting Christianity for their own gain. The next four varieties are less maliciously inclined, but that still doesn't negate the damage they cause.

• *Fire-Insurance Christians* scare easily, and though thoughts of hell may drive them to "accept Christ," they are always trying to find minimal salvation—just enough to get by. Their favorite question upon hearing what God wants of them is "Do I *have* to in order to still be saved?"

• *Creedal Christians* find salvation by agreeing with a prescribed list of truths. Our evangelistic strategies, or lack of them, have produced more of these than any other. The Four Spiritual Laws are the epitome of Christianity by creed. They forget that good theology isn't enough; it's how much of it we allow to shape our lives that is important. As James 2 points out, even demons can affirm correct theology: "You believe that there is one God. Good! Even the demons believe that—and shudder."

• *Good-hearted Christians* seem so loving, kind, and generous (at least externally) that even though they don't get "too religious" everyone assigns them believer status. They do little harm to Christianity itself, since they often demonstrate more kindness than real believers, but they endanger themselves by finding a false security in their perceived goodness rather than surrendering to Jesus.

* *Ethical Christians* try to find salvation by living a morally impeccable life, and outwardly they appear that way. Yet when this is produced by their own strength of will, it produces very little of Christ's compassionate character. These people are usually happy only when demanding of others the same ethic that makes their own life so miserable.

You can't find life in God with any of these attempts, and we've done a grave disservice to anyone who thinks such approaches give him security. People can't walk with God on their own terms. In letting them think so we've made the road so broad that it is meaningless. The number one reason why genuinely seeking people are turned off to the church is because hypocrisy lives unchallenged within it. And I can't blame them, for the road Jesus gave us wasn't nearly so wide:

> Enter through the narrow gate. For wide is the gate and broad is the road that leads to destruction, and many enter through it. But small is the gate and narrow the road that leads to life, and only a few find it (Matthew 7:13,14).

"Few find it" not because God has hidden it but because few want to pay the cost to be his followers. If any of the approaches above characterize your relationship with God, take note. That may be why his life is not as real as you thought it should be. But I have good news for you: There is a better alternative.

What Is a Christian?

We may think there are many varieties of Christians, but the Bible recognizes only one kind—disciples. Disciples are those people whose hearts burn with an unquenchable hunger for God, desiring to know him better every day. They are not perfect, but they keep pressing ahead to be changed into his likeness, and their lives are marked by a confident faith.

There are lots of people like this (you probably even know some), but regretfully they are often typed as exceptions. Yet they are not meant to be. They model what normal Christianity should be—following God with a whole heart. They should get all the encouragement they need, but unfortunately church programs are often designed to restrict them while accommodating people who see God's Word as an intrusion into their plans.

In defining conversion we have become too preoccupied with determining whether someone goes to heaven or hell. If we are so bored or pained by Christianity that the only reason we're going along with it is to escape hell, I'm afraid we miss the point. Jesus' message was "Repent; the kingdom of heaven is near." The glory of God's kingdom and his compassionate offer to share it with us is the motive needed to build disciples. We can have fellowship with God again, now and through all eternity.

The object of conversion must be to open people to God's presence and their participation in his kingdom. That takes more than praying a sinner's prayer or sitting in a pew every week listening to an anointed sermon. You don't add Christianity to your life like you join the Rotary Club—attend meetings and pay dues. Christianity redefines life itself under the lordship of Jesus Christ.

The rich young ruler was willing to be ethical to have salvation, but balked when Jesus asked him to give up the possessions he so dearly loved. Jesus calls us to love him with all our heart and to live every day in His presence. That's the joy of Christianity. If we really want heaven, we can live in pieces of it now, every day.

Coming to Christ

What do we really have to do to enter God's life? That's what the people asked Peter after his first sermon, and the answer he gave them still holds today:

> Repent and be baptized, every one of you, in the
> name of Jesus Christ so that your sins may be for-
> given. And you will receive the gift of the Holy Spirit
> (Acts 2:38).

They had just seen 120 people burst out of a room with
more joy than they had ever witnessed. They had just heard
from Peter's mouth that the Jesus they had crucified was in
fact the awaited Messiah, and they had each at the same
moment heard his sermon in their own native language. They
were hungry, and Peter gave them two simple steps to fill that
hunger.

First, repent. Everything about the way we live outside of
Christ is centered in our own desires, feelings, and needs.
That is the source of our sin and the arrogance that drives God
out of our lives. It produces trouble upon trouble.

To repent means to change your mind, to surrender uncon-
ditionally to the Father as the source of all life. Repentance
sees his gift of holiness not as God destroying our fun but as
God freeing us from the destruction of darkness. It affirms
Jesus Christ as Lord of all and yields to him total control of
every remaining day of our life.

Repentance is not a popular message and is too often
avoided. Chuck Colson tells us why:

> Repentance can be a threatening message—and rightly
> so. The Gospel must be the bad news of the conviction of sin
> before it can be the good news of redemption. Because that
> message is unpalatable for many middle-class congrega-
> tions preoccupied with protecting their affluent lifestyles,
> many pastors endowed with a normal sense of self-preser-
> vation tiptoe warily round the subject.[4]

Yet for us to enjoy intimacy with God we must be brought to
repentance daily, whether we're just getting saved or thereafter
freshly submitting our lives to God.

Be careful not to confuse repentance with regret. Regret is
sorrow over the consequences of sin. I've met many people who

are sorry they are going to jail, getting divorced, or running out of money. They regret the decision that contributed to their pain and are looking for help. But if that help is anything less than total surrender to Jesus Christ then it isn't repentance no matter how much they weep.

Bob was a confused young man. Nineteen years old, hooked on drugs, and wanted for theft, he showed up on the doorstep of one of the couples in our fellowship with his 17-year-old girlfriend. They were in despair and wanted help. Different ones in our fellowship spent time with them, and they eventually said they wanted to follow Jesus.

And they started to—until they found out how much he wanted to change them. Fearful that the changes God was making in them might change their relationship to each other, Bob backed off. Days later he tried to commit suicide. No matter how deep the pit, and how much we despair being in it, regret is not the same as repentance. Regret is self-centered even in its sorrow and cannot bring itself to submit to anything other than the whims of flesh no matter how much more pain it brings.

Repentance is proved not in the moment of anguish but in the actions that follow it. "Who warned you to flee from the coming wrath?" John the Baptist chided his self-righteous listeners. "Produce fruit in keeping with repentance" (Luke 3:7,8). That fruit is the humility of a life submitted to Jesus, no longer championing its own agenda but following God's.

Second, be baptized. "An unessential outward symbol" would unfortunately sum up the opinion of many about baptism. In the New Testament that act of obedience consummated people's desire to follow Christ.

"Look, here is water. Why shouldn't I be baptized?" The Ethiopian's words to Philip underline the depth of this conviction about baptism. This is not to say that the water holds any magic; it doesn't. It is *obedience to Christ's word*, not the water, that makes the difference. Being baptized because of peer pressure or formality is lifeless. Baptism is only as real as the surrender in our heart.

Baptism's importance cannot be discounted. Those who try to do so only prove otherwise by their refusal to be baptized. I've nursed along many new believers only to find them unwilling to follow Jesus if it means they must be baptized. Their problem with baptism may be no bigger than the embarrassment that comes from being wet in front of a group of people, but if they won't follow Jesus that far, they usually won't go much further either. Though I've met people with a vibrant faith who had not been baptized, their omission was on account of ignorance rather than refusal. Upon learning what Scripture taught about baptism, they willingly completed that step.

Peter tells us that these two steps, repentance and baptism, made in concert with each other and in sincerity yield two immediate benefits. The first is forgiveness of sins, what Hebrews calls a "cleansed conscience." The mind and spirit are liberated from failure and guilt. We feel like we've never sinned before and are free to confidently taste of God's presence. Fellowship severed by sinfulness is restored.

The second result is what Peter called receiving the gift of the Holy Spirit. The reality of God's presence floods our being in the person of the Holy Spirit. He comes to be our guide, teaching us how to know God better and how to follow his will. He also brings us power—to yield to God, to love, to heal the sick and raise the dead.

These two benefits take all the abstraction and ritual out of the conversion experience. The evidence of salvation is in the freedom of forgiveness and in the fullness of the Holy Spirit. That's how we tell when conversion is genuine—because that person becomes alive with God's presence.

This is salvation, and if you've never experienced intimacy with God, this is where you can begin. Find someone you know is alive in God to walk through these steps with you. Open your heart to God and know it is done when his power and presence floods your being.

Continuing in Christ

Coming to Christ genuinely is meaningless if we don't continue in him. Jesus drove home that point in one of his parables and gave us reasons why some people lose sight of their faith.

A man went out to sow a crop. As he threw seeds, some fell on the roadway and were eaten by birds, some fell on the rocks where they couldn't root (and withered when the sun came out), others fell among thorns where they were choked by weeds, and the rest fell on good soil where they flourished. Each of these shows us different ways we can be robbed of God's life and what we must do to ensure that our life with him will endure until he comes again.

1. *The word misunderstood.* Someone hears the gospel and accepts it, but because no one showed him how to walk out that decision, even what he had gets eaten away by the enemy. Unless discipleship walks hand-in-hand with evangelism, new converts are stillborn and end up frustrated and condemned by their own lack of growth. If this is where you need help, find a mature believer who will meet with you every week to answer your questions and teach you how to draw from God's presence.

2. *The word unheeded.* The seed on the rocks gets into the soil, indicating that it is understood, but the plant can only hug the surface. All is fine as long as it's raining, but when the rain stops, even briefly, the soil dries out quickly and the plant dies. As long as such people are healthy and happy they are fine, but they fall away amidst persecution.

I know that the word "persecution" evokes images of lions and stonings, but that's not entirely the point. Jesus is talking about hardship of any kind. Your faith in God needs to run deeper than your circumstances, or it will collapse when trouble comes—and come it will!

3. *The word ignored.* The third kind of seed grew up in the soil and rooted deeply. Alongside it, however, were weeds that grew up and choked it. These weeds represent the worries of life and the deceitfulness of wealth. I have seen so many growing Christians thwarted by the purchase of a new home, the birth of a baby, or simply trying to keep up with their credit card payments. Enthusiasm for God can be eaten away by the simple demands of everyday life.

This is perhaps the greatest danger for us in America, since we have so much to be distracted by. A pastor once lamented to me, "I'm not sure it's even possible for a middle-class person to be saved." Obviously he was overstating his concern, but he had seen many people start out well and then relegate God to a distant corner of their life. Wealth (or the pursuit of it) is extremely deceptive. We think we can have God and still work for the wealth of this world. Scripture says otherwise.

4. *The word obeyed.* If we can get past these three obstacles, our life in God can grow deep and rich. Rather than conversion being the greatest day of our life in Christ, it will be just the beginning. Every day we can grow to know him better and be more equipped to live in his glory and power. This is where the Word becomes fruitful, and as we feast on its fruit we experience joy almost greater than we can contain.

The chapters ahead are designed to help you get your life firmly planted in an intimate walk with Jesus. If you've never known that experience before, get started. If you've known it but have drifted, he is still waiting for you, wanting to share with you the joy of his presence.

It Is Not
Too Difficult for You!

7
When Did It Get So Complicated?

THE LOSS OF SIMPLICITY

Martha, Martha . . .
you are worried and upset
about many things.
—Luke 10:41

Even as I sit at my desk writing this chapter, a ravenous monster lurks not more than 12 feet behind me. He is big—ten feet across and eight feet high. His name is Library. In small doses he can be very helpful, but when he lines up all his strength against me, he can be quite formidable—even though he can't move an inch.

He's got eight shelves full of books of every size and description. Most I've read, some I've skimmed, and some are there because I still hope to read them. But each one calls to me with its own agenda. Here are five books with detailed blueprints for deepening my spiritual life. I have nearly two dozen books on the definitive church structure, none of which agree with the others except on one point—my church is doing it wrong!

I have a dozen books on human relationships and family life. I'm amazed that marriages even stayed together before the invention of the printing press. And I have 12 different slants on eschatological events, each using the same Scriptures to prove widely varying points of view.

I have workbooks that offer me ten easy steps to anything I want—but most of them don't work. And just try to prepare a preachable sermon with Augustine, Luther, Wesley, Finney, and Spurgeon staring over your shoulder!

But my selection of books on current issues is the most intimidating of all. I have 15 selections cheering me to more activity than I can produce in six lifetimes. Sell your home and live among the inner-city poor! Get rich so you can send

71

money to God's evangelists so they can help the poor! If God hasn't specifically told you to stay in America, go overseas as a missionary! We must stop abortion now! The list goes on and on—antipornography, New Age movement, politics, Latin America. . . .

Sometimes I want to rip this monster from my wall. It's not that I don't enjoy books, since my wall wouldn't be full of them if I didn't. But I get this nagging feeling that we've made Christianity far more complicated than its Founder intended. And I get that same feeling whenever I look at a church calendar or my own schedule, or attend a pastor's conference.

When our hearts cry out for an intimate fellowship with God that seems to escape us, maybe we ought to look at how complicated we've made a very simple gospel.

Busyness: The Complicating of Time

Have you ever planned an elaborate party and invited all your friends, only to have most of them back out at the last minute? You might even have sympathized with their excuses, but in the end you were still deeply disappointed. No one cared enough to make the sacrifice necessary to come.

Jesus told a story exactly like that in Luke 14. A man prepared a banquet and invited his friends. Then the excuses started. "I have just bought a field and I must go see it." "I have just bought five yoke of oxen and I'm on my way to try them out." "I just got married." The host of the banquet grew angry. He vowed never to let his first-invited guests come at all, and instead he invited the poor and the handicapped to his banquet.

In this parable Jesus wasn't talking about attending parties, but about partaking of God's kingdom. Busyness can keep even well-intentioned people out of the kingdom, and if that was a concern in Jesus' day it is obviously a crisis in ours.

Though on the average we work fewer hours than any generation before us, we are far busier. Our so-called leisure time quickly evaporates in the face of household maintenance, social commitments, recreation, and taxiing our children (who must be involved in at least three outside activities in order to validate our conscientious parenthood).

These opportunities are multiplied by the fact that we can drive 300 miles in half a day's time or whisk around the world by air. When we do have time left over we are too tired to do anything but fall in front of the mindless banter of television. There, sandwiched between our favorite shows, are slick appeals to even more busyness. Devised by the best minds of our time, they lure us toward even more leisure activities and entice us to buy even more possessions.

We've become a nation of activity junkies. Ask people how they are doing, and nine out of ten will find some way to let you know how busy they are. Though we complain about our busyness, we don't really hate it. If we did, we would stop it. Busyness does have its rewards.

It is easier to be busy than to be disciplined. Having no overwhelming purpose for existence, we compensate by filling time with things we think will make us happy. The enemy hardly needs to tempt the believer today with evil activities when he can distract him guiltlessly with so many neutral ones. The result is the same: The Christian still loses sight of the kingdom of God.

Busyness keeps us from making difficult choices. There's something easy about a day in which every waking minute is filled with running from one meeting to the next. "I don't have any time today" is a great excuse for not seeking the Lord for wisdom and not yielding to his priorities for the day.

Busyness makes us feel important. Who has ever seen an "important" person who is not rushing off with something else to do? When I get a phone call prefaced with the question "Are you busy?" I feel pressured to answer affirmatively lest people think they've caught me sitting in the office staring into deep space.

Busyness is the price of meeting everyone's expectations. Aunt Elma wants you at the family reunion, neighbor Bob needs you to help pour a patio, and there's a men's seminar at the church. Everyone wants a chunk of your time, and if you can't risk disappointing some people you'll be torn apart by their competing pressures.

How easy it is to forget that there is only one Person whose expectations we are to meet—Jesus! And he expects us not to be weighed down with busyness, because this has nothing whatever to do with fruitfulness. Jesus never evidenced a harried lifestyle, and yet at the end of his earthly life he could say to his Father, "I have brought you glory on earth by completing the work you gave me to do" (John 17:4).

Intimacy with God is found in a quiet and focused life. Hurriedness and clamor drown out his presence. Schedules always heighten the importance of pressing things and blind us to things that are essential to deepening our walk with God. Excessive activity keeps us too preoccupied to pay the price for an effective and lasting discipleship.

Yet the church, instead of addressing this sin, competes with it by hosting and prodding people to attend even more activities. Some churches host dozens of meetings each week and exalt those people who attend them all. Where are the quiet moments for enjoying God and his creation and the kind of deep conversation which arises only out of the spontaneity of unhurried encounters? How many moments like that have you had this week?

A couple of years ago, as I rushed across town from one meeting to another, a lonely man by the side of the road caught my eye. He was unkempt and looked so lonely. I was instantly filled with compassion for him and felt like I should stop and help him. But I drove onto the freeway anyway, lamenting the fact that I was already late and couldn't stop.

I didn't get away with it, though. That brief encounter haunted me the rest of the day. As I prayed about it later, the parable of the Good Samaritan came to mind. Every time I had shared from that parable I had railed at the priest and the Levite as hypocrites who had lost their compassion for people to the professionalism of ministry. I had never thought of them as compassionate people who might merely have considered themselves too busy to stop. We ask God to use us, but then we keep our lives so full of activities and meetings that he can't get an opportunity in edgewise.

Professionalism: The Complicating of Theology

The power of clergy over laity has always been a focal point of church reformers. Church leadership easily falls into the trap of validating their usefulness by placing themselves as an essential link to personal spirituality. Reformers have instead championed the priesthood of all believers—which simply means that every believer can have a personal relationship with God and be used by him to touch others. Leaders do have a distinct function in the body, but they do not have a relationship with God substantively different from that of other believers.

Never before in the history of the church has the theology of priesthood received so much lip service and so little actual practice as in this century. Though it is preached with conviction from our pulpits, only a small percentage of believers are involved in significant ministry opportunities on a daily basis. They may be doing lots of busywork for someone else's program, but they are neither thriving in their spiritual experience nor confident to intervene in crisis situations.

I would say that fully 90 percent of those who were already Christians when they came to our fellowship did not at that time have a daily time of worship and Bible reading which was effectively nurturing their lives. They had been accustomed to being fed by pastors and TV preachers. When opportunity arose to lead someone to Christ or to liberate them from oppressive bondage, they told them to see the pastor or come to church for their answers. We are breeding a generation of believers who perceive themselves as incompetent to live out the Word in their own experience.

How are we doing this? The church has historically used two tactics to keep people dependent on their leadership, and regrettably we have our twentieth-century versions of this today, subtle or unintentional though they be.

The first revolves around interpretation of the Word. Are the Scriptures clear enough for the average person to read and understand, or must they be interpreted by a professional? In the days of John Wycliffe this issue was obvious. The Bible was only available in Latin, which only the priests could read and interpret. The church killed anyone who translated it into common languages or who possessed translated copies. This they did in spite of the fact that the Holy Spirit used mostly unlearned men to pen his Word. The New Testament itself was written in the style of Greek used on the street, not the classical style used by scholars.

Today *misapplied* scholasticism serves the same purpose of making people feel like they can't understand the Word on their own. I'm not against the knowledge which the church has gained over the centuries nor using the original languages to help us understand the Word more fully. If, however, we use those tools week after week to say that though the text *seems* to say one thing it *really* says something else, we effectively destroy people's confidence to feed from the Word themselves. Good preaching doesn't dazzle people with interpretations of the Word that defy the imagination; instead it gives a fuller appreciation for the inherent simplicity of the Word. At the end of a good sermon people should respond, "Yes, I see that!"

The second tactic to keep the masses dependent on leadership is to make them a mediator in the salvation process. In the Middle Ages the church viewed the communion elements as the means of salvation—which only a priest could consecrate. The priest could withhold communion from anyone he chose to and thus in his mind deny them salvation.

We have long recognized that the whim of a man cannot determine salvation, but many people surrender the quality of their spiritual life to ministry professionals and become willingly dependent upon them. Later we'll take a closer look at this phenomenon, but for now we need to point out the adverse effect which ministry professionals can have on personal intimacy with God.

Instead of people sitting at the feet of Jesus themselves, hearing his voice and obeying his will, they sit at the feet of their favorite teacher. Public-relations techniques have produced a generation of leaders today who aspire to lead by their own personal popularity. We have our celebrities just like the world does, and many Christians are more awed by them than by the Lord himself.

Media use today has only heightened this problem. Instead of multiplying ministry through transformed people, we seek to do it through satellite dishes and direct mail. How ineffective these have proven to demonstrate God's love or to help people grow up in Christ! Some people can't make it through the day without a fix from their pastor's cassette ministry or a word from the TV evangelist they champion. In an age of "capitalistic Christianity," leaders only encourage such dependence: "You must hear what I'm going to talk about next week." "This series on growth will change your life like nothing else you've ever heard." Dependent people ensure the future of the ministry.

Even church-growth experts suggest that this kind of promotion and visibility is essential for church growth.[1] We've entered dangerous waters indeed when the promotion of a man's image is the means by which we extend the gospel. The Reformation did us little good if we only exchanged one pope for thousands of little popes through whom people try to live out a Christian experience.

No wonder people perceive themselves as incompetent to handle the situations in their life through personal knowledge of the Word, sensitivity to the Spirit, and support of the body! While our books on child-rearing were intended to help parents, often they do the opposite. I constantly remind discouraged parents that they do not need a degree in child psychology to raise their children. Any parent who takes a personal interest in his or her child is in a far better place to disciple and discipline that child than any outsider, no matter what the outsider's knowledge or experience. Though we can benefit from the insights of other people, we must be sure that they do not intimidate us.

In the same way, daily Christian living has become far too complex. Jesus chose the weak things to confound the wise. With all the principles and precepts that have been outlined in recent years, we need to ask ourselves whether we've kept things simple enough for the person on the street to walk with God in confidence. Jesus channeled a powerful gospel through the lives of fishermen, farmers, and former harlots. Walking with Jesus is within the reach of every individual, for he makes us competent to walk out the gospel in our own lives (2 Corinthians 3:4,5).

Protocol: The Complicating of Relationships

The worst thing about getting married is enduring the dating ritual. I hated it. Every date is a constant guessing game of each other's feelings. Every nuance is evaluated and reevaluated. Should I hold her hand? Does she like me? Should I give her a good-night kiss? Would she go out if I asked her again?

In dating such complications may be unavoidable, but it seems we've let all relationships become that complicated. The most thought-demanding aspect of our lives has become what others think of us and how we should relate to them. Protocol and public relations are two factors that add to this complication.

Our society is governed by written and unwritten rules of protocol—what you can and can't do in every imaginable situation, most of it depending on the "pecking order" of our society. To breach your assigned position is unthinkable, even when doing so would greatly enhance the work of the kingdom.

Jesus knew no such restraint. No one approached people with greater compassion, yet when the situation called for it he could take whip in hand and clear the temple of those defiling it—even though they were the religious leaders of the day. Elsewhere he called them hypocrites and even rebuked his own friend with "Get behind me, Satan!" He disappointed his closest friends by not rushing to their side at Lazarus' sickness.

We are so bound by protocol that it is difficult for us to rescue someone we see drifting away from God. We think it is none of our business.

How many times have you seen your brethren growing cold in religion, and have not spoken to them about it? You have seen them beginning to neglect one duty after another and you did not reprove them in a brotherly way. You have seen them falling into sin, and you let them go on.[2]

These words of Finney seem to break all forms of protocol, and if you know anything about Finney's ministry, you know he often did this very thing. For some reason it is more acceptable today to gossip about someone's failure behind their back than it is to confront them with it.

Public relations has added another complicating factor to relationships by placing more effort on how we appear than on what we really are. My copastor serves on a school site council which was once about to be evaluated by a state team. To prepare the council, the principal went over the questions they would be asked and the answers they should give. My friend stopped him and suggested that instead of worrying about the right answers they should be honest about what they were really doing and be evaluated on that basis. The suggestion was met with incredulity.

Corporations use such PR to sell their products, and people use it to sell themselves. Image is more important than substance, and we can even come to believe we're something we're really not. Lukewarmness spawns in such waters. In fact that very model is being offered today as a basis for Christian growth. Confess your personal success until you convince yourself it's true—whether it is or not.

Trying to foster the right image distorts the honesty and integrity which our relationships need in order to promote spiritual growth. Whether we're praying, worshiping, or sharing, we can easily be more concerned with how we're appearing to others than with whether we're really getting to God's presence and being shaped by his life. Images are hard to live up to, and that's why God calls us to be genuine: It even allows our unhealthy places to be available to God for healing.

No wonder we end up with relationships pocked with pressure, anxiety, and identity crises! What we know about each other is too often only a fabrication, and protocol keeps us from facing that fact.

The life of Christ was never intended to become so complicated by busy schedules, intricate theology, or pressure-filled relationships. Jesus made it so simple that anyone he touched could understand it enough not only to transform his own life but also to pass it along to others.

Aren't you tired of rushing through life and missing out on moments of peace and refreshment in God's presence?

Aren't you sick of feeling incompetent to make the gospel work in your own life as well as in others who want help?

Aren't you ready to give up trying to be whatever someone else wants you to be or lying awake at night wondering why Joanie gave you the cold-shoulder on Sunday morning? Don't you want relationships with other believers that are full of forgiveness, encouragement, admonishment, and affection?

> In repentance and rest is your salvation, in quietness and trust is your strength (Isaiah 30:15).
>
> The fruit of righteousness will be peace; the effect of righteousness will be quietness and confidence forever (Isaiah 32:17).

Isaiah knew that God's life doesn't flow in the complications of life. When you turn your back to such complexities, you'll find that intimacy with God is one of the simplest things you can learn.

8

Simple Intimacy

RESTORING SIMPLICITY

I am afraid that . . .
your minds may somehow be led astray
from your sincere and pure
devotion to Christ.
—2 Corinthians 11:3

Perhaps some people would find life more enjoyable if it could be faced with outlines and pie charts, but preferences actually make little difference, since life doesn't come to us in definable doses. Start any week with a balanced allotment of time for family, job, church, and recreation and it's sure to fall apart by noon Monday. Even though I border on being a schedule-holic, I'm grateful for that phenomenon. We weren't designed to live like robots. Even the best-laid plans of regimentation, in schedules or theological priorities, never fully rise to the plateau where love, joy, and beauty reside.

These do not flow from the bondage of objective order, but out of sincere and pure devotion to Christ. He knows the demands of each day and the needs in our lives far better than we do. If we willingly follow him, we will find time and energy enough for our work, family, spiritual growth, and meaningful relationships—yes, even for ministry and rest! In Christ our frantic busyness, our feelings of incompetence, and our pressure to please people can be healed. That freedom is one of the choicest fruits of intimacy.

A Personal Relationship with God

Tim Stafford created a fictitious character, Joe, to describe what happens to too many people when they are invited to become Christians. "He walked down front expecting a personal relationship with God. He left with the understanding that he must read the Bible and pray every day. No one has explained very precisely the connection between the two." Joe studies the Bible and gets involved with a church, but a seething disappointment underlies his activities, "the discrepancy between what he was offered—a personal relationship with God—and what he actually experiences."[1]

I've met many people like that. Their desire for a personal relationship with God, and perhaps even a taste of it, drew them to Christianity in the first place. They were ignited by the glory of his presence and were overwhelmed by the depth of his love. But they never learned how to grow in their walk with God, and eventually it was drowned in a flood of religious activity. They either abandoned Christianity, disillusioned that it didn't live up to its promise, or revised their expectations to fit a lifeless pattern of attending church functions. Either way, they discounted their initial experience as emotionalism.

But God's desire to be personal with you has never changed. I have already used the word "intimacy" to describe it, for I can think of no better term. The word itself conjures up the romance of tenderness, the safety of privacy, and the joy of comfortable familiarity, all of which characterize the relationship which God wants to share with you.

In the last two chapters we talked about bringing Christianity out of an abstract theological plane in order to make it a real part of everyday life. This is essential to intimacy, for it doesn't happen without our conscious participation. Intimacy means that we live with a sense of God's presence and that our hearts and minds respond to him throughout the day.

Two important aspects of intimacy will help us keep his presence out of the abstract. First, God wants to communicate with each one of us. Prayer was never intended to be a monologue in which only our concerns are expressed to God. He also wants to give us his wisdom and direction. Jesus said that one of the major assignments of the Holy Spirit was to mediate this dialogue: "He will guide you into all truth. . . . He will speak only what he hears, and he will tell you what is yet to come" (John 16:13). In coming chapters we will look at how God speaks to us and how we can grow in our sensitivity to him.

Second, God wants to share his power with us. Human effort alone will not accomplish God's work. Unless he fills us with his love, we will just exploit people for our own ends. Unless he fills us with peace, our path against the current of the world will destroy us with anxiety. Unless he gives us the power to heal human hurts, how can we convey the depth of his love?

What I love about the church's prayer meeting in Acts 4 is not only that in the face of persecution they saw their need for boldness, but also that they got down on their knees until God filled them with it. They did not contrive a six-step plan to greater boldness. They did not institute persecution practice. They sought God because they knew that only he could make them bold.

The term "spiritual gifts" is often used today to refer to God's supernatural working through people. Though too much focus on this term has caused some problems, God does want to use you as a channel of his power. He wants it to be that practical, and Peter Wagner correctly identifies that lack of power as a major problem for believers today.

> Ignorance of spiritual gifts may be a chief cause of retarded church growth [in North America] today. It also may be the root of much of the discouragement, insecurity, frustration and guilt that plagues many Christian individuals and curtails their effectiveness for God.[2]

I know that many evangelicals are tormented by such definitions of intimacy that include God speaking to us and sharing his power through us. Of course God is active today, they admit, and as long as that activity lies beneath the surface of human observation, they have no problem with it. Though he is real, they say, we can't feel him. Though he can convey his will by inner impressions, they can't bring themselves to say that he speaks to us. Though he can give us courage to endure cancer, he can't heal it.

> The deepest and most healing human relationships always involve touch. This fact, however, introduces some sadness into our relationship with

God, for we do not touch him. The popular chorus
"He touched me" is religious hyperbole. It reveals a
longing for God's touch, but nobody has actually
felt God's hand.[3]

We talk about knowing God but deny him access to any part
of our anatomy except the mind and any tool except the Bible.
How unfortunate! God wants to touch us, and though this is
more often felt by our heart than by our skin, I find it no less
discernible and far more real. Why would we expect God, a
spiritual being, to touch us in the same way other humans do?
Though he uses visual appearances or audible voices on rare
occasions, only science limits us to our five senses. Scripture
makes clear that our link to spiritual reality is through our
heart or spirit and not our senses.

God's regenerative work at conversion makes our heart
alive again to his presence. He wants us to expect his presence
to be real: "Anyone who comes to him must believe that he
exists and that he rewards those who earnestly seek him"
(Hebrews 11:6). He rewards us with himself. This is our inher-
itance under the new convenant.

A Theology of Intimacy

The very fact that God speaking today to people seems
awkward to our Christianity should concern us deeply. We've
lost a theology of intimacy, and with it the practical presence
of God which it releases to the believer. This is both the proof
and the cause of our nakedness. Having lost the goal of New
Testament Christianity, we are adrift in its terminology and
practices. In fact, much of church program today is little
more than old-covenant experience disguised in new-covenant
terminology.

No passage more succinctly describes the heart of the new
covenant than Hebrews 8:9-12. The writer quotes Jeremiah
31, stating that it was fulfilled by Jesus' death on the cross and
is now in force.

This is the covenant I will make with the house of
Israel after that time, declares the Lord. I will put my laws

in their minds and write them on their hearts. I will be their God, and they will be my people. No longer will a man teach his neighbor, or a man his brother, saying "Know the Lord," because they will all know me, from the least to the greatest. For I will forgive their wickedness and will remember their sins no more.

This covenant stands in direct distinction to God's old covenant, and establishes the foundation of intimacy with God.

Instead of motivation and direction coming from without—through laws, creeds, and religious observances—it is meant to flow from within, from his laws written on our hearts and minds. We are free from meeting all the religious expectations of someone else's rules and programs; now we can pursue our own personal relationship with God.

Instead of God manifesting himself as a mysterious and fearful presence lurking behind the veil, terrifying his people into subjection, he would live within us as a friend and guide. We become his possession, cared for with a depth of compassion reserved only for sons and daughters.

Instead of God revealing himself to just a few people, he would now reveal himself to all. No one needs a priest, prophet, or even pastor to tell him what God is like, for we can all know him personally, "from the least to the greatest." Secondhand revelation—living off someone else's relationship with God—is no longer necessary. We can each find God to be more real to us than our best friend.

How is this marvelous intimacy possible? The last verse in the quotation makes it clear: The new covenant is based on God's mercy, not our performance. The other characteristics show us why the new covenant is better, but this one shows us how it works. The law depended on human effort, which was never good enough to bring us into God's presence. Under the new covenant God's justice was fulfilled by Jesus' substitutionary death.

The focal point of this mercy is forgiveness. The old covenant provided for forgiveness, but it was primarily intellectual. Certain rules were given, and if they were observed the person could trust that his sin had been atoned for. But Hebrews 9 tells us that the ceremonies could never make perfect those who draw near to worship. In other words, the sacrifices were only a stopgap measure, for the forgiveness was only ceremonial. The conscience remained tainted by guilt.

In Christ's sacrifice, however, the cleansing is fully effective. His forgiveness cleanses our conscience so that we can stand before God as if we had never sinned. Because we are that clean, we can come before the awesome, holy God with confidence, assured that we belong there and stand ready to partake in our relationship with him.

Growing in Intimacy

Though the second half of these chapter-couplets are designed to help you grow more intimate with God, I must admit at the outset that building intimacy is something that God does with us. It would happen very simply in each of us if we didn't allow ourselves to be distracted from its pursuit, or restrict God's moving by false expectations.

Jesus in John 15 compares our relationship with him to a branch drawing life from a vine. Growing results from simply abiding in him, which we do by loving him and drawing near to him. He is the source of our fruitfulness. Without him we will not be able to do anything. With him we will be full of his life and fruitful in his kingdom.

I'm reminded of this fact every time I lead worship. God's Spirit will move freely and powerfully among a group of people who are submitted to him. I can do far more to mess that up than I ever can to produce it. I only have to follow God's agenda and ensure that I'm not forcing my own ideas in order to have an effective time in his presence.

You'll find the same thing in your life. As you open your heart to him, he will teach you all you need to grow in him. All you need to do is stay simple enough and trusting enough to follow him.

The following suggestions should prove helpful. It's a list that I review often, especially when my own touch with God is not as real as I know he wants it to be.

1. Your submission to God is the key that unlocks God's presence to you, not just at conversion but also every day thereafter. "Masters die at the Master's coming,"[4] or at least they need to. God's presence will not flourish where it competes with other priorities. He is not our means to fulfill selfish ambitions, nor does he offer his counsel as mere advice to be evaluated.

Cultivate a heart that surrenders to God about everything in your life. Submit specific parts of your day to him, willing to obey whatever his wishes are. Submission actively seeks God's leading; it doesn't sit back and take life as it comes, assuming that God's will is done automatically. As Finney said, "Do not confound submission with indifference. No two things are more unlike."[5]

2. Keep your heart humble before God. Though Scripture tells us to come confidently to him, we cannot forget that our friendship is between two unequals. He is farther above us than we are above ants. Pride blinds us to that and ultimately to God. It puts self at the center of our life, and there God cannot be seen.

3. Go to God continually. A branch draws from the vine all the time. It does not walk away, only coming back when it needs a fill-up. It is always there, drawing from the vine. In our walk with Jesus a weekly or bimonthly touch with him just won't suffice. We need to touch him every day and meditate on him throughout the day.

4. Stay with it even when it seems difficult. I said that intimacy was simple, not easy. Jesus warned us that forceful people break into the kingdom, because your own flesh and the flow of the world will always try to pull you away from God. You won't always be excited at the prospect of spending time in his Word or meeting with God's people. Often when you pray your mind will be bombarded by extraneous thoughts. Just relax and with God's grace press through the distractions. You'll always find God's presence worth mining for, and when you come away from being touched by him you'll wonder why you weren't excited to get there in the first place.

Many believers fall short of discovering intimacy because they make their walk a matter of convenience. If you allow them to, the needs of work and family obligations, as well as the desire for leisure, will never let you walk with God. If your walk of faith is like a yo-yo, it is usually because you are worshiping, studying, and participating in body life only when you feel like it or when you have nothing better to do. That will never lead to intimacy.

5. Finally, all our pursuits must be predicated on grace. After times of failure and neglect, you need to know that God is still waiting for you, ready to wash you with forgiveness and set you back on the road to his life. We will never earn the goodness which God pours out of his life into ours; we can only receive it with a depth of gratitude that offers our own lives back to God as living sacrifices. As you grow in intimacy you will find yourself constantly drinking at the fountain of his grace, where forgiveness and strength nourish our lives.

The Building Blocks of Intimacy

There are three very practical places where we can experience and extend our intimacy with God. I'll warn you that these are familiar places. I doubt that anyone who has been around the church much hasn't been told to worship God, study the Scriptures, and have fellowship with other believers. We all know we should do these things.

The problem is that we either don't do them consistently enough or else haven't discovered how to make them effective. I want you to look at these disciplines not as tasks which we must complete but as places where God wants to make himself known to you. Our goal is to keep them alive, never being satisfied with just having put in our time.

Often when I begin reading the Word, it seems like little more than ink on the page. I'll finish a chapter and can't remember a thing I read because my mind was racing a hundred other directions. You know what I do? I start the chapter all over again. I have simply determined not to stop reading the Word until I've got something out of it that can affect my day. It may be a new insight about God, an attitude he wants to heal in me, or a greater grounding in my faith. I've read some chapters five times in one sitting before I fulfilled my objective.

With that goal in mind, let's take a fresh look at these important building blocks to intimacy.

1. *Worship.* Worship at its height is an *exchange* of love and communication between the Father and his child. It usually begins with adoration but only reaches its peak as God reveals himself to us. Though great strides have been made in the last couple of decades toward a refreshed understanding of worship, the focus has largely been in getting to God's presence, not on what to do once we're there.

Once we've come into his presence, he wants to interact with us, speaking words of love, affirmation, direction, or concern or giving gifts of peace, rest, or faith. Far from static adulation, worship is a dynamic conversation between a Father and his child.

If this kind of personal worship is new to you, don't get hung up on form. God wants you to present your heart to him in simplicity and honesty. Here are some suggestions to help you get started.

- Set aside at least ten minutes every day to be with the Lord.
- During that time get alone, away from distractions (TV, children, phone calls, etc.).
- Begin by seeking God's forgiveness for the sins and failures of the preceding day.
- As you sense his cleansing, begin to praise the Lord. Sing a familiar chorus, read part of a psalm, or express how you feel about him out loud, in your own words.
- As you do that, keep a tight rein on your mind if it begins to wander to other concerns of the day. Bring it back to God.
- Once alive to his presence, enjoy the conversation: Pray about your concerns; listen to his; relax from the

world's pressures in the safety of his presence; intercede for others or receive insight for the day.

If we're having daily times of worship in which God has our undivided attention, then we'll find it easy to extend worship throughout the day. Brief moments of prayer while driving, working, or conversing with others will become much more effective.

Genuine worship makes us alive to God's presence. Of course he is always with us, but this time of worship helps us partake of that presence. Just as I am with my children as I sit in the family room and watch them play, my "being with them" takes on deeper meaning if I am actually interacting with them, either by conversation on the couch, going for a walk, or joining their game on the floor.

2. *Bible Study.* The most effective tool to learn about God and his ways is the Scriptures. Anyone who genuinely hungers for God will be a person who studies the Word, because it is a complete revelation about God's own nature and his plans for us. True intimacy doesn't devalue the Bible's importance, since it is the only validation we have for our experiences with God.

Read the Bible every day as part of a devotional time incorporated with the worship and prayer time we mentioned above. Start small. I'd rather see someone spend ten minutes a day in the Word that is meaningful for him than fight boredom for 30 minutes. Eventually ten effective minutes will grow to 20 or 30 minutes because the reader is hungry, and not because he is trying to fulfill an obligation.

Choose a translation that is easy to read. Paraphrases may be good for overviews, but they are not as accurate as translations which have been scrutinized by a wide range of scholars. The New International Version or the New American Standard Bible are excellent study Bibles.

Have a plan in the Word and stay accountable to it. Sometimes I read large sections for a wide-angle view while at other times I read only a chapter or paragraph for more concentrated meditation. Prayerfully think about what you're reading; ask God to show you something that will benefit your growth and obedience to him that day. This makes the Word a practical aid for our life in God and will save us from the trap of going away from the Word stimulated intellectually but not shaped spiritually.

Study aids can be excellent tools, but don't become dependent on their charts or commentary. Read a passage and think through it yourself first, and then read the extras for further insight. Have confidence; the Word was written for you to understand!

3. *Fellowship.* Subsequent chapters will deal more extensively with this area, but we must include in this context the importance of sharing with other believers. It is a bountiful source of encouragement, balance, and help.

Christian fellowship is so much more than polite conversation at a missionary tea or looking at the backs of people's heads in the pews in front of you. Biblical fellowship means that people share together out of what Jesus is doing in their lives. They serve each other even when it is inconvenient, are honest with each other even when it is difficult, and pull together instead of pulling each other apart. Most people don't understand the difference between this and attending church services, and that is tragic because these two things have little in common.

Find two or three other believers with whom you can meet regularly. Worship together, share insights from the Word together, and support each other through prayer and practical service.

On Learning Intimacy

Even though I can share some key principles about intimacy with you, it is not easily taught by classroom lecture or book instruction. It can only be learned by doing it yourself with someone who can guide you in your discoveries.

America has put too much stock in classroom learning alone, and the church has followed suit. Not all things can be taught that way, and intimacy is one of them. When I was 16 I took flying lessons. There is a lot you can learn in a classroom about flying—navigation, weather conditions, aerodynamics, and what the instruments are for—but one thing you can't learn is how to fly! That takes a one-on-one experience in which an instructor sits by your side for some 60 hours of flight time, showing you step-by-step how to do it, watching your every move, and correcting your mistakes quickly.

Too many Christians have never gotten out of ground school. They know all *about* Christianity but very little of how to actually walk with God. What they need to know can't be taught by a lecture, but only by someone who will personally show them. If we do it for pilots, how much more should we do it for disciples? Jesus did. He invested hundreds of hours in just a few men—but those men really learned how to do it.

If you're serious about intimacy, find people you know who have a closer walk with God than you do, and ask them to help you. Meet with one of them weekly, sharing what you're learning and where you're struggling. Listen responsively to their suggestions.

Intimacy with the Almighty God is almost too awesome to contemplate. Our minds will never contain all that he is. Paul said our intimacy is like a poor reflection in a mirror; we only see glimpses of him. Though the promises are great indeed, and though we must pursue them with all we have, we must not be frustrated when their fulfillment is not yet perfect. Our finite frames cannot handle God's complete revelation, nor our minds his greatness.

Growing in intimacy is a lifelong journey, and the best is saved for last. One day, clothed with immortality, we will behold him face-to-face!

Letting God
Be God

9

God in a Box

THE LOSS OF SPIRITUALITY

---

*My people have exchanged their Glory
for worthless idols.*
—Jeremiah 2:11

The dust of the battle still hung in the air, mingled with the smoke and smell of burning sacrifices. Overturned tables littered the temple court. Doves fluttered through its columns. Coins could still be heard rolling across the stone floor, and people were still scurrying to find them.

In the middle stood Jesus examining the damage. The merchants pressed toward him, demanding an account for this sacrilege. "What gives you the right . . . ?"

"Destroy this temple and I will raise it up in three days." He was calm but resolute. The merchants surely snarled in confused anger. It wasn't enough that he had just destroyed their use of the temple; now he wanted to destroy the whole building! If they doubted before that he was mad, they did so no longer.

"How can you raise up in three days what took 46 years to build?" The suggestion so angered them that three years later they raised it at his trial and taunted him with it as he died. John tells us that the temple Jesus spoke of raising up was his own body, which he did three days after he was crucified.

But his words of destruction were still directed at the physical building in which he stood. For the temple was more than just a misused place of worship; it was the heart of a theological system unworthy of the new covenant which Jesus had come to inaugurate.

The temple represented God in a box, neatly packaged and removed from the mainstream of human experience. This is not what God intended when he gave Moses plans for the tabernacle. He wanted them to know that he lived among his people. Jesus now wanted them to know that God had come to live in them.

So he challenged them to destroy the temple—if not the building itself, then at least what it had come to convey. His warning dare not escape us, for it seems that we all find God easier to live with if we try to box him in a tidy package.

> [We] have always bound God to temples, festivals and ceremony. Evil priests found power in controlling the All-powerful. And frightened people were happier not bumping into an arbitrary God unawares. But even when fraud and fear were *not* motives, people believed that the limitless had found limits and *therefore* was approachable.[1]

It happens so easily. We seek God so desperately when we need something from him, but conveniently exclude him when pursuing our own ambitions or wisdom. We want him nearby, at church or in our private devotions, so we can get to him when we need him, but we don't want him lording over every area of our lives.

We also try to hide from God's transcendent nature beneath our definitions and rules. God in a box is systematic theology at its worst. We use our knowledge of him to limit his greatness, confident that we know what to expect from him in any situation. Our rules of conduct are so carefully reasoned out that we can follow them, never needing to touch him or hear his voice.

Though such things make for a safe religion, they rob it of its vitality. Much of today's Christianity has become exactly that: external rituals and codes of conduct "having a form of godliness but denying its power" (2 Timothy 3:5). The outside of our lives may look wonderful, but inside we are empty. When we need God's power we try to draw it from him but find ourselves unable to do so.

A spiritual person is not one who can memorize theological facts, conduct his life with flawless ethics, or busy himself with church programs. A spiritual person is one who has learned how to walk in the Spirit, following his voice and being a vessel of God's character and power.

God in a box is religion without God's presence, without spirituality. It is people moving by works for God instead of God moving through his people. It is idolatry of the first order.

Idolatry in a Scientific Age

> Their idols are silver and gold, made by the hands of men. They have mouths but cannot speak, eyes, but they cannot see. Those who make them will become like them, and so will all who trust in them.

Ancient cultures were filled with idols, and these words from Psalm 115 depict three characteristics of them. First, they were manufactured by people. They had no power or virtue because they were only a fabrication of the culture, with qualities and rules to fit their needs. Those cultures that carried little guilt had benevolent gods which only needed an occasional festival to keep them happy. Cultures ravaged by guilt needed something more painful to appease their inner pain, so they introduced blood sacrifices. Idolatry allowed people to construct their own religion.

Second, they were lifeless, not able to speak or do anything practical to help their followers.

Finally, even though idols were inherently powerless, worshiping them did change the worshiper. People become like the idols they worship. If their gods were demanding, the people became demanding. In this case their gods were blind and deaf idols, and likewise Israel had become deaf to God.

It's difficult to find similar idols today. Some say we make idols of our homes, cars, and TV's, but I don't think so. The Israelites had tents, camels, and other kinds of recreation, but this was not called idolatry. Even when someone coveted gold and silver, it wasn't called idolatry but greed.

Our idols have to meet the same criterion as theirs: lifeless entities of our own devising that change us by our trust in them. To find our idols today we need to assess the difference between our cultures. Idols made of stone and precious metals were spawned in an age of superstition when everyone accepted the idea that events were controlled by unseen spiritual forces. Western culture, with the rise of scientific thought, no longer accepts this idea.

Robert Jastrow, a science laureate, explains how science has become the basis of religion in our age. "The principal element of that religion [science], or 'faith,' is a belief that everything that happens in the world has a scientific explanation, for every effect there is a cause. It is not a supernatural cause, but one physics can explain and understand."[2]

Our culture bows at the altar of physics, so you could expect our idols not to be gods of stone but principles of thought. Though their philosophies differ, most people are convinced that if they live their lives a certain way, definable results will follow. The primary focus is on human effort. Even Christianity has not escaped this adverse effect of rationalism. It has lowered our view of the transcendent God and made us less dependent on his power working in our lives. We can change ourselves by understanding the right principles, we can heal ourselves through medical technology.

But even science warns us that such philosophical views push science further than it claims to go. Jastrow warns us against accepting scientific conclusions without question: "There is no proof [that physics can explain everything]. In fact, I think there are questions in science that are beyond our reach at this time."[3]

Nonetheless our laws of cause-and-effect have produced the idols of our age. They are our false religions, putting people's confidence in their own abilities. We will not take time to examine the false religions of this age. Any that leave out the one true God are obviously wrong. Our greater danger comes from those idols that retain allegiance to the God of the ages but distort his real nature. Cloaked in Christian terminology, they trick people into thinking they serve God when it is only a god of their own creation, shaped by their own desires and needs.

That's what the Pharisees faced at the temple and what we risk today. We, like them, can easily cower from seeing God as he really is, preferring to think of him as we want him to be, predictable and controllable.

Today's God-Boxes

I doubt that any of us are untouched by the temptation to limit God's moving in our life. To help us find out how this is so, let's look at a few popular idols that line the shelves of our intellects today. These are what we must destroy if we are going to let God freely live within us.

The ritual box. God is a distant presence who only wants to be honored by patterned worship and lifestyles. Days and years consist of religious observance, but, like the idol-worshipers of old, we expect him neither to speak nor to actively come to aid us. Since his presence is not the object of our worship, we often end up using our religious observances for our own gain, like the Pharisees fasting to be seen of men rather than heard by God. Who of us in praying publicly hasn't thought more about the people listening than the God whom we're addressing?

The fairy godmother box. God exists for our pleasure. Whenever we have a need we can run to him, expecting him to wave his hand and make everything better. This kind of god always hears *our* concern but is rarely listened to for *his* concerns. He might ask something of us that we don't want to do, and that's not what fairy godmothers are for; they exist only to give us what we want.

The Burger-King box. God will do it our way. We treat his truth like a smorgasbord, thinking ourselves free to go through the line and pick out which parts we want and to ignore what is distasteful. This is consumerism at its worst because it makes truth relative to our own desires. It can only result in our deception. Flannery O'Connor was right: "The truth does not change according to our ability to stomach it."[4]

The generic box. Make God's life cheap enough to fit the masses. Churches today compete for attendance by making

Christianity as watered-down as possible: Come to church, put a little money in the offering plate, and be good. Such churches never face a call to discipleship that befits the Lord of glory and transforms their lives.

The self-help-box. Ben Franklin may not have invented this box, but he certainly popularized it: "God helps those who help themselves." Our ingenuity and hard work can make good things happen for us. Robert Schuller seems to agree: "You can be anything you want to be, you can go anywhere if you are willing to dream big and work hard."[5] You are the master of your own destiny; God only helps out as a silent partner.

The formula box. This box is the most evident result of scientific thought on theology: We serve God by obeying principles. If we'll do steps one, two, and three, God responds in a predetermined fashion. Consequently we have six steps to a more vital prayer life, five steps to deal with anger, four steps to lead someone to Jesus. But this results in legalism and reduces our actions to mere incantations, with our hope in our own performance.

The "God-told-me-to" box. Popular among charismatics, this box allows us to pursue our own ambitions by stamping them with God's endorsement. It's amazing how many people today God has called to be rich and famous, and how few he has called to self-sacrificing ministry!

All of these boxes compromise God's transcendence over our lives. So why do they each have their adherents? Whether by promise or by chance, they do motivate people to action, and those actions can produce temporal results. Extra effort can make significant temporal changes for many people, but they cannot bring salvation, nor do they endear God to work on our behalf.

These boxes are designed to "sell" to the masses, offering quick temporal results for the strong of will. But even those they help are maimed spiritually, for they never learn to trust God, to hear his voice, to submit their lives to his ways and find true life. Instead, they become like the god they worship—full of empty promises, legalistic demands, and lifeless words.

The Temple of the Living God

Even though we've added all these new God-boxes, to a large extent we've kept the old one too. Though I've not yet seen a church building with a "holy of holies," we still talk of our church facilities as "the house of God." Often we impute a reverence to the sanctuary itself, somehow believing that God visits this place especially. Sunday school literature still applies the familiar "I was glad when they said unto me, 'Let us go into the house of the Lord' " as an admonition to church attendance.

> When it comes to *church* buildings—often mistakenly called "houses of God"—whatever critical faculties we have are further blunted by a sacralist mentality which says expensive buildings are justified because they are dedicated to religious purposes or "God's glory." Surely God deserves the best! We forget that God does not live in temples made with hands. . . . The community of God's people is the temple of God, not our fine structures of glass and concrete . . . little sanctuaries where we wall off God from the world.[6]

I suspect that our preoccupation with building expensive facilities for God's glory may be less a matter of theology than it is an excuse for opulence. Either way, the glorious truth is that God does not live between glass and concrete, and we would do well to stop pretending that he does.

He lives inside people, and our attention must be directed at making them the temple of God—vessels prepared for his presence and walking worthy of the God who inhabits them. Imagine what would happen if we gave as much attention to *individual* lives as we give to our buildings—how much healing would result, how much transformation!

Do you see why Jesus was so passionate that morning at the temple? If he couldn't break the mentality of God-in-a-box, he couldn't inhabit their lives, which is exactly what he wanted to do. This is true spirituality, the transcendent God living in us, involved in our affairs and leading us to an abundant life in his love.

How does that prospect look to you? If it's anything less than the most exciting opportunity that has ever been offered to you, then you do not understand who God is and what he wants to do in you.

The thought of being a temple of the Lord, Paul said, makes everything else in this life look like the rubbish it is. His ultimate passion was to know Jesus in the power of his resurrection and the fellowship of his suffering. Who in his right mind would not want to live every moment to the will of God? Haven't we had enough time to prove that our own ambitions, while perhaps carrying some temporal benefit, are nonetheless destroying us?

Instead of pushing God away from us into our own boxes, let us welcome him with open arms. His desires for us are "immeasurably more than all we ask or imagine" (Ephesians 3:20).

Who's in the Box Anyway?

Before we leave this discussion, let's take one last look at our God-boxes. Do we really think that the God of the Ages could be encased in a box of anyone's making? Of course not!

He is God, after all. What building can contain him? What principle can fully define him? What deception can thrust him out of our lives? How foolish we are to ever think so!

So when we create a box to wall ourselves off from his presence, just who really ends up in there? We do. We cannot contain God, but we can limit his moving in our lives by refusing to honor him as God.

And that, I think, is what hell will be. It is the final box where the wicked can wall themselves away from God. C. S. Lewis said, "I willingly believe that the damned are, in a sense, successful rebels to the end; that the doors of hell are locked on the inside."[7]

Believe me, you need no protection from God! Yes, he is awesome and powerful, and certainly that can be threatening.

But he is not an unknown power, for he has demonstrated his love to us in Jesus, by sacrificing his life so we could be saved. How can we ever doubt the intentions of a God who loves us that much?

10

Intimacy and Dependency

RESTORING SPIRITUALITY

My sheep listen to my voice;
I know them, and they follow me.
—John 10:27

The funny look on my daughter's face caught my eye as I walked through the family room. She was guilty of something, but what? She was obviously in pain, and obviously trying to hide it. "Are you okay?" I asked.

"I hurt my finger on the TV." She held her finger out to me, her face twisted with the cry she didn't want to let out.

I walked toward her. "How did you do that?"

"I pinched it." On the end of her index finger stood a fresh white blister.

"How could the TV do that?" As I looked up I saw our wood stove just behind her. "You touched the fireplace, didn't you?"

Once the facts were out there was no need to restrain her anguish. She exploded into screams and tears. My wife ran to get some medication. I hugged my daughter tightly, and as I pressed her head against mine I offered up the parent's lament—"How I wish you could just trust me, honey, when I tell you something!"

I wonder how often God has wept over me in the same way. How much hurt have I endured because I wouldn't listen to him or trust what he told me? But, like my daughter, sometimes I think I know better.

David understood how foolish that attitude is, and in Psalm 28 he expressed just the opposite:

> To you I call, O Lord my Rock; do not turn a deaf ear to me. For if you remain silent, I will be like those who have gone down to the pit.

David needed God's involvement in his life every day. He refused to accommodate his life to God's silence and instead sought him earnestly. His desire to please God placed him in situations greater than his own ingenuity or strength could resolve; often his failure would have meant his death. It was this dependence that called the young shepherd boy to face a lion unarmed, Goliath with only a few stones, and eventually the throne of Israel.

If a spiritual person is one who relies on God's Spirit, obeying his direction and drawing his power, then dependency is the essence of spirituality. No greater challenge lies before anyone than the adventure of learning to depend on God, and no greater treasure will ever be discovered than the reality of God's presence that such dependence produces.

Need God? For What?

It may be easier to see your need for dependence when you're standing face-to-face with a bear or going out to battle the Philistines than when you're enjoying the material comfort and safety of twentieth-century living, but the dangers are no less acute and the potential for destruction is no less real.

Society and technology have combined to greatly reduce many of the risks that previous generations faced daily. Regular paychecks supply our needs. Weather forecasting, irrigation, and food storage provide an abundance of food even if the weather is uncooperative. Many illnesses have been cured or controlled, and costs for treating them are insured. Social programs help meet the needs of the poor and unemployed.

As a result, few people today have an immediate sense of needing God. Though our coins say "In God We Trust" and we passionately sing "I Need Thee," too many people think only in the abstraction of a distant Sovereign who quietly keeps the world together and secretly blesses our efforts. Our own efforts work so well so often that it is difficult for us to see how desperately we need God.

Only occasionally does this veneer of false security shatter, usually by personal tragedy. Unemployment, incurable disease, catastrophic accident, or emotional darkness intrude on the best-laid plans. Funerals of close friends or relatives call our temporal priorities into question and show them to be what they really are—sand castles, providing only an illusion of security. They are destined to melt without trace into the next passing wave. How swiftly our wealth, health, prestige, and friendships can vanish into circumstances beyond our control!

In the back of our minds we know the tide can turn quickly, but for the most part we do not lie awake at night worried about getting our next meal or being assaulted by a neighboring tribe. Tragedy is comparatively rare, and even when it occurs most people manage to recover fairly quickly and get on with life. At least for the moment, for most of us our material needs will not drive us to depend on God.

But this doesn't mean that our needs are actually any less real than David's—only less obvious. When we gather everything the world offers, we find it insufficient for the cry within which we thought it would satisfy. Spiritual emptiness and despair can be masked by work and play only so long. When we look behind the facades we see a battle raging all around us. Sin and evil stalk our planet, tearing people apart and driving them away from God.

As long as we are only concerned with our material comfort, few of us will ever learn how much we need God. But if every day our goal is to please God in all things and to demonstrate his love to the people around us, we'll see how much we really need him.

The Case Against Dependency

Dependency is not an easy attitude to cultivate. We have an arsenal of excuses to defend ourselves against it.

1. *I want to do it my way!* The old nature doesn't give up just because we surrender our lives to Jesus. Every day it will test our will in an attempt to regain control of our life. Our flesh at its root is selfish and independent. I do what I do because I want to, it makes me feel better, and I don't want anyone telling me otherwise. Its theme song is "I Did It My Way."

But the flesh isn't always that obvious. It can even couch its desires in religious terms. Even in many Christian circles, self-reliance and self-assertion are encouraged for the believer. Jesus warned us that even though we aim for his life, these methods will miss that target: "Whoever wants to save his life will lose it, but whoever loses his life for me will find it" (Matthew 16:25). Spiritually, few things take the obvious route.

The intimacy which God extends to us will never come as the culmination of self-effort, but only as the abandonment of it. Though it will always be easier to do something on our own for God, without consulting him, listening to him, and obeying him, we must resist that course. The flesh's quest for security and comfort must be abated if we're going to be free enough to obey him. This is difficult to learn for a generation that has learned to avoid risk at any cost through its insurance policies and extended warranties.

2. *Only flaky people live that way*. It seems that everyone knows somebody who got excited about God and decided to "live by faith," which means that he stopped working and lived off others who were working. Others have even waited for a word from God before they brushed their teeth. It is also true that people who begin a statement with "God told me . . ." often finish it with something stupid: They are going to be rich or they need to build another building.

But these bad examples shouldn't prevent us from finding true dependence on God. Being dependent on God doesn't make us irresponsible; it just adds a new dimension to our responsibility. Instead of responding to our own desires, we respond to God's; instead of trusting our limited knowledge and observations, we gain God's wisdom.

This doesn't mean, however, that those who don't understand God's wisdom won't mock your decisions. Charles Finney had an apt warning for those who would live full of the Spirit:

> I never knew a person who was filled with the
> Spirit that was not called eccentric. . . . They act

under different influences, take different views, are moved by different motives, led by a different spirit.[1]

3. *I tried to trust God before, but he let me down.* This may be the most difficult barrier to cross. Just about everyone has a story of a desperate moment when he cried out to God but was disappointed in the response. Why didn't God heal my mother? Why was I unemployed for two years even though I prayed every day? I suspect that for every soldier miraculously saved when he cried out to God for help, many more weren't. Only a fool would put his life in the hand of a friend who has failed him on a previous outing. And for many people trusting God feels exactly like that.

Trust for God, however, isn't built by looking at past experiences. They are too easy to misinterpret. There are many reasons why God may not have dealt with a situation as we thought he should, but the Bible makes it clear that he never responds to us with less than absolute love. That's where dependence is grounded.

Remember, we began this book by saying that the church is naked. We can't take the experiences of a captive church and make them a commentary on God. We can't live our lives by our own wisdom and then in a moment of crisis expect to throw up a request at God and demand that he answer it. He does want to be intimately involved in the needs of our lives, but this happens only as we walk with him.

4. *It won't work for me.* To the self-condemned, dependence always sounds like an unreachable dream. But if it works only for those who grew up in middle-class homes with godly parents, then it is not the gospel. It must also work for the prostitute, the victim of child abuse, the poor, the uneducated. And it does!

The door is open to all of us. Don't let the enemy's personal accusations keep you from entering it. God wants to teach you how to depend on him effectively. That's the essence of the discipleship which Jesus taught to all kinds of people.

Jesus' School of Discipleship

When I look at how little Jesus' disciples seemed to understand, I wonder what he did with all the time he gave them. Even though Jesus clearly told them about his death and resurrection, they tried to talk him out of it, and did not even remember what he had said until after it happened. Even on the day of his ascension they were still asking if he would now restore the kingdom of Israel.

Though he didn't teach them the theological facts which our twentieth-century bias would anticipate, he did teach them how to depend on God in every situation. We can see it best if we focus on how he dealt with one of those disciples.

The first time they met, Peter was cleaning his nets from a night of fruitless fishing. Jesus asked to borrow his boat so he could teach the crowds from off shore. When he was finished he told Peter to go out a little further and drop the nets. Peter resisted, since even with his best efforts he had already come up empty. He finally consented, though, and how much fun it would have been to see the look on his face when the net began to wiggle under the weight of his unearned load! Though this was the greatest catch of Peter's life, he never sold it. He walked away from it to follow Jesus.

Later, on that same sea, the disciples were caught in a violent storm. Afraid for their lives, they awakened Jesus, and to their surprise he rebuked the storm and it subsided. But Jesus took them further. "Where is your faith?" he asked, hinting that God could have done the same through them.

To make his point clearer he sent them out on their own. He told them to take no provisions, heal the sick, drive out demons, and preach the kingdom of God. On this evangelistic campaign media hype and flamboyant oratory would not suffice. The disciples needed the power and presence of God.

When they returned, Jesus sought to take them off alone, only to be pursued by a crowd of 5000 people. After he ministered to them all day, he told the disciples to give them dinner. Again he called them to think past their own efforts, and by a word of blessing he fed the crowd with a little boy's lunch.

On another occasion the disciples couldn't drive a demon out of a small boy. Jesus prayed for him, staying with him through violent convulsions until he was free. When they asked him why they were unable to free him, Jesus explained that the situation demanded more prayer than they had given it. They asked him how to pray, and he taught them to make sure you pray according to God's will, and when you do so keep seeking until you break through every obstacle.

Jesus' itinerant lifestyle gave him ample opportunity to demonstrate how God can provide for his children. One time he even told Peter to get some money from the mouth of a fish. Even as Jesus' life drew to an end, the lessons continued. He sent Peter to prepare the Passover meal, and everything that Jesus told them in advance came to pass. Even before Peter denied His Lord, Jesus already saw the failure and encouraged him to get up after it was over and then return to strengthen the other disciples.

Jesus' brand of discipleship was profound. It dealt less with facts than it did with total dependence upon the Father. Through every need, failure, and joy he showed them that God's wisdom and power were sufficient.

Did they learn the lesson? Their last recorded words to Jesus in the upper room demonstrated just how well: "Now we can see that you know all things and that you do not even need to have anyone ask you questions. This makes us believe that you came from God."

Jesus responded, "You believe at last!"

They had come to the end of their own reason and resource. They saw Jesus as the one to whom they could totally entrust their lives, not because he compelled them to but because he really did have all wisdom and power. If anything, the disciples learned this lesson too well. That's why they couldn't understand the cross nor his ascension. They had become so dependent on him that they couldn't imagine life without him.

They had yet to understand the power of Jesus coming to live in them through the presence of the Holy Spirit. Jesus told them about it, but he wasn't bothered when they misunderstood, for he knew what would happen on the day of Pentecost.

What we see in those disciples from that day forward was not only the result of the Spirit's presence but also the fruit of their learned dependence on him. That's what took them to the farthest reaches of the Roman Empire announcing the coming of God's kingdom, healing the sick, and enduring persecution.

Proverbs calls this dependence "the fear of the Lord" and says it is the beginning of all wisdom. This fear is not terror that makes us run and hide from God but a fear of facing anything in this world if God is not with us. That attitude is essential for us to pay the price of intimacy. Again and again we come back to him as the only thing we can depend on.

"I Need Thee!"

"I feel like God is saying to me that he's going to teach us how to trust his power more than we now trust our own efforts." I still remember the morning Gene shared that thought during one of our Sunday morning services. Though the promise in that statement excited me, I also thought how unbelievable it sounded. I prayed about situations because I knew I should, but I honestly didn't see where it made much difference. My own scheming and fretting seemed so much more effective.

Over the next year, however, God fulfilled his promise in our congregation. Whatever we did by our own efforts began to unravel, and we saw how unfruitful our efforts were in really filling people with God's life. On the other hand, things that we sought God about, waiting to act until his will was clear, were changing quickly. I'm still enjoying the transition which God made in my life that year. Where I used to intuitively trust my own wisdom, I now find myself praying earnestly—not merely because I should, but because it is the only thing that brings enduring change.

Growing in dependence is the essence of spirituality, and Jesus will lead us to it as he did his own disciples. Two kinds of experiences will be important here. First are those times when God provides for us or uses us in ways that are so special that we are overwhelmed by his greatness and goodness.

Second, he uses those situations in which we are challenged by need so great that we know we are powerless to resolve it ourselves. Don't despise those moments or blame God for them. Paul tells us he doesn't create them (our godless world does that) but he does use them to draw us to deeper dependence. "We were under great pressure, far beyond our ability to endure, so that we despaired even of life. . . . But this happened that we might not rely on ourselves but on God. . . . He has delivered us from such a deadly peril, and he will deliver us" (2 Corinthians 1:8,9). Don't run from situations that make you totally dependent on him, for that's when you're the most open and pliable to his work.

Both of these kinds of experiences will encourage you to draw near to God every day. Trust doesn't just endure circumstances while hoping for a favorable outcome. It hears God's voice in their midst and obediently follows him until his goals are achieved.

Hearing God's voice is essential to trust or else it will degenerate into mere presumption. When I take my kids to the mountains, they know they can trust me. I'm not going to let anything harm them, let them get lost, or fail to rush to their attention if they need help. To have the benefits of that trust, however, they must stay within earshot of my voice. If they wander too far away they won't be able to hear me.

There is a variety of ways in which God speaks to us. First Corinthians 2:11-13 tells us that the Spirit inserts his thoughts into our minds. Some people refer to this as inner impressions or a still, small voice, but it is God speaking. Suddenly a new thought fills our mind with direction, wisdom, or even rebuke.

Scripture is another source that God uses to speak to us. Not only do we gain general knowledge from the Word, but often during our reading a specific Scripture will just reach up and grab us by the eyes and say, "Look here!" God uses that inspiration to help us face something for our life or equip us for the day.

The Bible gives us many other examples of how God communicates—an audible voice, dreams, visions, and even angels. Admittedly these are more rare, but they are nonetheless tools at his disposal. Sometimes he communicates without words, instantly overwhelming us with a sense of his love, peace, worship, faith, joy, or boldness. Times like that make us keenly aware of his intentions toward us. He also uses other people to talk to us, with or without their being aware of it.

In all of these, however, we must look to hear his voice. Just because we have a thought or dream, or someone tells us "God told me to tell you . . ." this does not mean it is God speaking. As we grow closer to God, his voice will become more distinguishable and we can move in it with greater certainty. Later we'll discuss ways that God has given us to confirm his voice.

For now, let God speak to you in a variety of ways. Rely on him and don't let fear of moving beyond your abilities keep you from following him. That's where fruitfulness is. Generally speaking, we are too preoccupied with staying safely in the limit of our own abilities, and because of this we do not learn how to depend on God. We try so hard to protect people from making mistakes that we deny them opportunities for growth. What Gordon MacDonald said about developing leaders applies to all believers:

> Currently there is a tendency in some Christian circles to create clones rather than leaders. There is very little room in our present evangelical climate for men and women to experiment. They stifle new ideas for fear of being labeled a heretic or having support cut off. Leaders must be molded in situations where they have the freedom to be wrong.[2]

Obviously he wasn't talking about experimenting with unbiblical ideas, but of people being able to follow God's leading without other people trying to pull them back to the safety of past procedures.

Don't be discouraged when God may not meet your expectations in a given circumstance. Instead, go to him and find out why. Were your expectations wrong? Did you just not endure in prayer long enough, like the disciples with the demon-possessed boy? Were you not close enough to God to hear him lead you through the situation?

Andrew Murray gave us perhaps the best direction for times like this:

> Learn to say of every want, and every failure and every lack of needful grace: I have waited too little upon God, or He would have given me in due season all I needed. And say then too—"My soul, wait thou only upon God!"[3]

Living every moment dependent upon God is what he wants to teach you. Submit to the risk of it and learn the joy of it. That's where you'll discover the deepest joys of intimacy with God.

Keeping Your Eyes on Jesus

11

Golden Shepherds

THE LOSS OF RESPONSIBILITY

Then we will be like all the other nations,
with a king to lead us and to go out
before us and fight our battles.
—1 Samuel 8:20

The car was packed and I couldn't wait to get started. I was leaving home to begin my freshman year at college, free at last from the final restraints of adolescence. As I was saying my goodbyes, my father pulled me aside.

"For 18 years I've been responsible for you. I haven't always been right, but I did the best I knew how. But now you're going off on your own and I can't be responsible for you anymore. I'm turning you over to God. You won't answer to me anymore, but directly to him."

The joy of my impending freedom quickly vanished under the seriousness of this new procedure. Until this time I had only to worry about my parents catching me when I did wrong. They were much easier to fool than God. I had never before realized the buffer I had let my parents become between God and me. Even though I was certainly accountable to God before that moment, the full weight of it sank in with my father's words. At the time it wasn't good news because I only thought of God as someone who enforced his rules at the expense of my happiness.

In the context of intimacy, however, coming before God without a human mediator is not only good news but it is what intimacy is all about. Knowing someone who knows God is not the same as knowing him firsthand, and God wants each of us to know him personally.

Firsthand friendship with God, however, has been all but abandoned in our current application of church leadership.

119

More often than not our pastors and leaders have become surrogate parents, standing between us and God. While we're busy about our jobs they seek the Lord for us, and our Christian experience is nothing more than doing what they tell us. God never intended it to be this way.

Give Us a King

This problem is not new. It seems that people have always tried to hide from God behind someone else. When the children of Israel saw God descend on Mount Sinai and set it ablaze with his glory they told Moses, "Go near and listen to all that the Lord our God says. Then tell us whatever the Lord our God tells you. We will listen and obey."

That same motive was also behind Israel's cry for a king. The excuses they used to beg Samuel to appoint them one (1 Samuel 8) are the same ones we use today to justify our own "kings."

"Then we will be like all the other nations." Everyone else had a king, so they wanted one too. Today we look at football teams with their coaches, corporations with their chief executives, and armies with their generals. Strong leaders are effective. Virtually every ministry organization looks to put a charismatic leader at the helm, developing programs and motivating people. We never question whether God has any better way than the world.

"[We will have] a king to lead us." Many people would rather follow a man they can see than the invisible God. A human king seems to provide the best of both worlds: Where he has good ideas we can follow him because we're convinced we're serving God, but when we disagree with him we can rebel with the rationalization that he's just a man. What does he know anyway?

"[We will have a king] to go out before us." Let someone else take the risks while we stay safely and inactively in the background. I suspect that the thought here may be less of having someone to follow than of having someone as a guinea pig, like sending your older brother out in the dark first. If the boogeyman is there it will eat him instead of you.

"[We will have a king to] fight our battles." Regretfully, God's army is overly staffed with mercenaries. Those putting in the most effort are getting paid for it. They even beg for the privilege, if we'll send them our money. At a fund-raising banquet for a rescue mission that point was stated clearly: "We feed and clothe the poor so you don't have to."

Many TV evangelists take that thought even further. Here's an excerpt from a fund-raising letter sent by an international charismatic ministry:

> [God] instructed me to open up my ministry to partners to increase its effectiveness. So, I began to receive partners. . . . Then he told me, "All of the people that are saved, all of the people that hear my voice through radio, television, tape ministry and all these other areas, your partners will receive the same reward."

Who wouldn't find it easier to write a check for ten dollars a month if that's all God asks of them to help extend his kingdom?

Because their hearts were so hard, God allowed the Israelites to have a king even though he knew the real reason. "They have rejected me as their king," he told Samuel, and how his heart must have broken! They preferred to follow a man instead of God himself. So do many believers today, and unfortunately they never find a shortage of men willing to let them do it.

Today's Royalty

Maybe our kings are not as obvious as the chariot-perched, gold-encrusted warriors of Samuel's day, but we have them nonetheless. They are only less obvious because we have so many of them. The nature of the church today allows us each to chose our own king, one who will provide the kind of leadership we want.

Our kings take three forms.

1. *Celebrities.* Just like the world, the church today is caught up in the exaltation of personalities. The media parades before us a large selection of preachers and singers. People become more infatuated with them personally than with their message. Magazine editors know that this is true. Many readers want articles on their favorite leaders more than those on Christian growth. The magazines that sell the best often feature a well-known personality on the cover. We even have our own media awards and popularity polls.

What may begin as a genuine response to God's gift in someone's life can subtly degenerate into hero worship. Driven by their own personal emptiness or inactivity, people seek to live out their faith vicariously through their favorite Christian personalities. They watch them constantly, send them their money, weep over their family crises, and even defend them ardently when their immorality or financial impropriety are revealed.

Not all celebrities encourage this fixation, but many do. They exploit their status for their own gain and they rule by their own ingenuity. Under the guise of anointing they prove themselves masters of crowd control and group dynamics, but do not demonstrate that they themselves are mastered by the Lord Jesus Christ. They are preoccupied with buildings, popularity, money, and media time, confusing these with ministry itself.

And not all of them are on TV; they can also reign in local churches. The distance afforded in a large congregation often promotes a similar infatuation with a famous or powerful pastor, a fixation that can supplant a person's own relationship with God.

2. *Dictators.* Many churches today, particularly charismatic ones, are led by a pastor who exercises personal control over the church and the people in it. Though power in the hands of a God-fearing man may not cause great destruction, few men wield such power without succumbing to the desire to manipulate people for their own gain.

This structure has risen from a misunderstanding of biblical leadership, assuming that a physical man has to represent the headship of Jesus. Where Jesus is not alive in the congregation I can understand why some people might fall for such an error, but if people are listening to him and being changed by him, no such structure is necessary. The Word offers us no precedent for one man ruling the local congregation. In fact John condemns the ministry of one man who projected himself into that spot in Ephesus (3 John 9,10).

Robert Girard in *Brethren, Hang Together* tells us why:

> The church is to be the expression of the personality of Jesus Christ, not the expression of the personality of any man. No single member of the body is to be allowed to leave his personal imprint on all the church's life and work. The church is to be dominated by the Spirit of Christ flowing through many lives.[1]

A pastor-dictator is the most direct form of kingship today. He tells the people what God wants of them, and all they have to do is cooperate. The congregation is always of one mind, because only one mind is allowed to function. Though this system makes for efficient congregations, it destroys the personal freedom and accountability needed for spiritual intimacy to flourish.

3. *People-pleasers.* Charles Colson quotes an assistant of a renowned media pastor. When asked to give the key to his man's success he responded without hesitation, "We give the people what they want."[2] He is not alone. There are many who succumb to this temptation. Micah's cry against the priests of his day applies to these leaders as well: "Her priests teach for a price, and her prophets tell fortunes for money" (Micah 3:11).

These kings rule by the scepter of their own personal popularity and ability to entertain the crowd. They may gather a large following, but their efforts are fruitless for God's kingdom. Nothing distorts the gospel faster than changing it to appeal to people's desires.

Though we must expose those who try to harm young believers by their need for personal power, most "kings" are as much a victim of the system as the people themselves. The system can even hide itself under the terminology of servant leadership, convincing its victim that all this is necessary to accomplish God's will. Many Christian leaders are well-intentioned though insecure people whose drive for personal affirmation can lure them into playing the crowd or pressing themselves to greater productivity.

Instead of challenging such weaknesses the church today caters to them. People want a buffer between themselves and God, but we must not let them have it. As a pastor, I'm always on guard for signs that people are becoming more dependent on my gifts than on Jesus himself. I know it is easier for them to do what I tell them, but if I rob them of hearing from God themselves, I've stolen the joy of intimacy. My task is to teach them how to draw on his life and to make Jesus the only King in their life.

The Seduction of Power

Even though God gave Israel a king, he warned them of the consequences. Power is intoxicating, and any brief illusionary benefit which kings provide is soon outweighed by the toll they take. We're not listening any better than Samuel's generation.

"He will take your sons and make them serve." And they did so, not just in legitimate wars to protect against their enemies but also to serve the personal whims of the king. Our kings today exact that price by alienating our sons and daughters from serving God. Congregations led by kings rarely transfer the excitement of the parents to their children because the next generation will prefer their own king.

I once asked a pastor, who was committed to the idea that the leader of a local church represents Jesus to that congregation, what would happen to the church when he leaves or dies. "It will die too," he said, apparently resigned to the fact. The future of our children should be motive enough to give up our kings and look for more biblical patterns of leadership.

"He will take the best of your fields and vineyards . . . and a tenth of your flocks." Kings must live in comfort, since daily concerns distract from their ability to lead. So we don't mind if our favorite TV preacher puts three phones in his master bath and pays for it with the widow's mite. There is no outcry at our celebrities staying in 4000-dollar-a-day hotel suites while they cry for people to sacrifice to help their ministry. One evangelist talks of going "to the desert to pray," never telling his viewers that it's to his estate in Palm Springs.

Kings also require money to appease their insatiable desire to extend their influence. But they always find other people to pay for the cost of their dreams. Those who help them are handsomely rewarded, but those who don't (or who express concerns about their tactics) are treated harshly. Micah spoke of such men:

> This is what the Lord says: As for the prophets who lead my people astray, if one feeds them, they proclaim "Peace"; if he does not, they prepare to wage war against him (Micah 3:5).

"You yourselves will become his slaves." The freedom of the life of Christ is lost to the programs and rules that a king-leader passes down to his people. His concern may be to minimize abuse and create the most efficient environment for ministry, but it enslaves people away from the joy of living with Jesus himself.

Part of the joy in the early days of the charismatic renewal was the realization that the Spirit wanted us to be a variety of vessels to accomplish his work. Believers were tired of sitting in the pews watching it happen on the platform. Yet how quickly we've returned to the same format in the name of keeping together our superchurches!

Why are we so blind to the corruption that accompanies increased power and influence? A look at Israel's kings demonstrates how few escaped it. Even the ones who started out with sincere hearts for God were ensnared in the trappings of power—Saul, Solomon, Uzziah, just to name a few. Only the strength of David's love for God saw him through similar corruption in his own reign.

The list grows in our age. Many good men, who launched out with a God-given call and vision, have been swallowed up by the seduction of power. Suddenly they find themselves in the midst of an organization that struggles to stay afloat. Their desire to follow Jesus in simple obedience has long since given way to the pressing problems of their institution. In the name of pragmatism they find themselves doing things they condemned when younger. They treat employees harshly and beg money from outsiders—all in the name of keeping the ministry alive.

The vision they began with has dried up and their joy within is gone. They can't find a way back to it without jeopardizing the monster they've created. Though subtle, the corruption of power and influence is unrelenting. It leaves many people spiritually empty and it can even drive some to compensate for the loneliness of their exalted position by indulging their flesh in opulence, financial impropriety, or sexual sin.

This is the result of having no qualifications for leadership except a man's own ability to raise money or garner followers. Today no demand is made of our leaders to show evidence of their integrity, maturity, or purity.

The PTL Network scandal of 1987 is only the tip of the iceberg. Many more such scandals will follow if we do not refuse ourselves the forms of leadership which God has denied us. Jesus said, "You know that those who are regarded as rulers of the Gentiles lord it over them, and their high officials exercise authority over them. Not so with you" (Mark 10:42,43).

Consumer Christianity

In a word, kingship leads to exploitation, even if those involved don't intend to do so. It stifles the growth of hungry believers and it alienates the world from hearing the gospel. Nothing has turned off this generation more than people who use Christianity to play political power games for the exaltation of their own ego and charge the poor for it.

That may not sound pleasant, but it shouldn't come as any surprise. When only a few years old the early church was already being exploited by such leaders. Paul was amazed not so much by the fact that it was happening, but by how much the people enjoyed it:

> In fact you even put up with anyone who enslaves you or exploits you or takes advantage of you or pushes himself forward or slaps you in the face. To my shame I admit that we were too weak for that! (2 Corinthians 11:20).

Not all exploited sheep are miserable sheep. Though it leaves many feeling abused and empty, many others are willing to tolerate the costs for the empty gospel it produces. These are responsible for our kings, because they have rewarded their appeals. They like leaders who strut like royalty with their Rolex watches and preach a gospel of ease and complacency. They will pay someone to fight their battles for them as long as they don't have to get involved themselves.

They are just like the people of Isaiah's day who refused to let the prophets face them with their own needs and failures. "Give us no more visions of what is right! Tell us pleasant things, prophesy illusions. Leave this way, get off this path, and stop confronting us with the Holy One of Israel!" (Isaiah 30:10,11).

Paul warned us that the church would face similar temptation: "The time will come when men will not put up with sound doctrine. Instead, to suit their own desires, they will gather around them a great number of teachers to say what their itching ears want to hear" (2 Timothy 4:3).

What other age could fulfill this prophecy as easily as ours? Today's media has provided us exactly that opportunity. We pick out the teachers that say what we want to hear, and then we support them with our attendance and money.

When I'm asked why so many Christian television programs distort the gospel, my answer is simple: The television gospel must be one that people will pay millions of dollars a year to hear. Humanity has never regarded truth itself that valuable—only a perception of truth that leads to personal ease.

We get the gospel we pay for and the men who can be paid to teach it. The result is a Christianity preoccupied with power, money, buildings, and organizations instead of the person of Jesus and his compassion for hurting people.

A Cry For Relief

"When that day comes, you will cry out for relief from the king you have chosen." These were Samuel's final words before he gave Israel the king they demanded.

That cry can be heard today. The exploited cry out in the emptiness of their spiritual lives, offended by the unrestrained egos of those who profess to be God's teachers. The hungry cry out for a more effective gospel that can transform them from within and fill them with God's presence. The mature cry out to be more than spectators in a program, but equipped to let the life of Jesus flow through them.

I've heard that cry from many people in recent years, and I've also heard it from Jesus. He has begun to expose and remove those shepherds who have held his people captive, and I expect that work to continue. It is time for his judgment to fall on our land, and it will begin first at his house. He wants to be our only King, and in him there is no abuse or insensitivity.

The words God used to chastise the shepherds of his people in Ezekiel 34 are no less appropriate for us. They may be words of warning to some, but to the hungry they are promises that God has something better in mind.

"Woe to the shepherds of Israel who only take care of themselves! Should not shepherds take care of the flock?" Instead of letting leaders feather their own nests with riches and influence, God will call forth leaders that will put the flock first. The day of the hireling is over.

"You have not strengthened the weak or healed the sick or bound up the injured." God wants his shepherds concerned with healing the wounded and bruised. That happens through individual contact, not through efficient programs.

"You have not brought back the strays or searched for the lost." It seems that the only people we search out today are the rich and powerful. One of our most popular TV evangelists had so much compassion for one of his listeners that he made numerous trips to San Diego to comfort her in the waning moments of her life. It sounds incredible until you hear the punch line: His organization inherited more than six million dollars from her estate! God is looking for shepherds who will not use his flock for their own gain but will love everyone, regardless of his or her position or status.

God ends his rebuke of the shepherds by saying that he will raise up one Shepherd who will love his sheep, caring for each of them personally and bringing them into the fullness of God's life. He has fulfilled that in Jesus, and you are welcome to come to him directly instead of going through someone who professes to be his broker. In fact, that's the only way you can come.

12

Intimacy and Accountability

*Clothe yourselves with the Lord Jesus Christ,
and do not think how to gratify the desires
of the sinful nature.*
—Romans 13:14

It's coming. As surely as the sun rises in the east, each one of us will face it and face it all by ourselves. It is nearer now than when you began to read this chapter.

> We must all appear before the judgment seat of Christ, that each one may receive what is due him for the things done while in the body, whether good or bad (2 Corinthians 5:10).

You will personally stand before God, stripped of all pretense and self-deception, without one thing to hide behind.

That may terrify some people. Hebrews 10:31 says, "It is a dreadful thing to fall into the hands of the living God." But that comment was addressed to those who deliberately continue in their sin after opening to the life of Christ. If I were one of those, I'd be scared too.

But it can also be a marvelous thing to fall into the hands of the living God. For those who have walked with God in this life, no day will be filled with greater joy. We will finally see him whom we have loved so deeply and be rewarded in his presence for our obedience to him.

As the apostle Paul came to the end of his life, he was not at all apprehensive but was excited about that moment he would come face-to-face with Jesus.

> I have fought the good fight, I have finished the race, I have kept the faith. Now there is in store for

> me the crown of righteousness, which the Lord, the righteous Judge, will award to me on that day—and not only to me, but also to all who have longed for his appearing (2 Timothy 4:7,8).

Many people mistakenly believe that the cross negates this moment of accountability. They think that Christ's blood washes our slate clean no matter how we've lived in this life. The cross was not designed to cancel judgment but to qualify us to meet its demands. It does this not by compelling us to meet an external code of righteousness but by changing our heart. In Christ we are declared holy before we do even one righteous act. But this judicial purity will also transform us into Jesus' image. We please God not because we have to but because we want to.

Later we will examine closely this amazing process, but first we need to see its importance and why our own individual responsibility to obey Jesus is essential to growing in intimacy.

Expedience: The Enemy Within

We said earlier that intimacy with God is not a difficult thing to learn. It happens quite naturally for people who love God and are surrendering their lives to him, but this is far easier said than done.

The difficulty in walking close to God comes from an enemy within—our own flesh. Though this old nature will allow us the pretense of Christianity, it squirms with discomfort at God's presence and will do anything to keep us from him personally. That's why it is so hard to build a consistent devotional life, to worship God openheartedly, or to press into meaningful fellowship with other believers.

While those things may be important for our growth in intimacy, they are also the undoing of our flesh. It just won't stand still for them and will try to keep us from them by making us too busy, too tired, too comfortable, too depressed, too happy, too anything so long as it keeps us from following God. It is so easy to fall victim to our old nature because it assaults us where we're the most vulnerable: appealing to our personal expedience. What's in it for me? Will I have fun? What will cause me the least trouble? The flesh provides these questions, knowing that temporal expedience is almost always gained only by compromising God's desires for us.

It can even provide us with mitigating evidence to justify actions we know aren't consistent with God's desires. Though we'll affirm his will easily in most other cases, our flesh convinces us that in *this* case we are an exception. Such reasoning has been behind believers marrying unbelievers, carrying anger in their heart, and not participating in body life with others.

Many well-meaning believers have never learned to challenge this self-pleasing nature. Realizing how powerfully we are motivated by self, much of Christian thought in recent years has been redesigned to appeal to the interests of the flesh.

The pursuit of God, however, can never be launched or propelled by expedience. Though God always looks out for our highest good, our flesh tries to prevent us from participating in it by highlighting its immediate costs. It offers us temporal pleasure at the expense of deep and abiding righteousness, peace, and joy.

If you want to grow in the knowledge of God you cannot appease the flesh but must allow it to die—every day. Peter found out about this when Jesus told his disciples of his impending torture and death at the hands of the religious leaders in Jerusalem. Peter tried to stop him: "Never, Lord! This shall never happen to you."

Peter couldn't reconcile Christ's suffering with salvation. Jesus was his teacher, provider, and friend. He could only see how much he would lose if Christ were gone. He thought he could save himself by keeping Christ from the cross, not realizing that to succeed in his effort would have denied him his ultimate goal. Self blinds even well-meaning hearts.

Jesus rebuked him harshly: "Out of my sight, Satan! You are a stumbling block to me; you do not have in mind the things of God, but the things of men." That's why expedience cannot participate in God's life: It values man's objectives above God's.

Jesus gave Peter a three-pronged attack on the enemy of expediency.

1. *"Deny yourself."* Galatians 5:17 tells us that our sinful nature will always be in conflict with the Spirit so that we are not free to act by our wants; they are too deceptive. But neither does this mean that we do the most miserable thing we can think of. Self-inflicted pain is also a response to self, and it has no value in drawing us to God.

We lay down our preferences as only the first step to hearing God's will and obeying him. Whenever I face a decision with competing pros and cons, the only way I can find God's will is after I set aside my vested interest in the outcome. When I can honestly say, "It doesn't matter, Lord; I'll do whatever you want," it is so easy to see what he wants.

Many people fear listening to God that closely because they can only imagine him sending them to the jungles of Colombia or to 14-hour Bible studies. God is not against pleasure, but only against the flesh's use of it to destroy us. If I'm playing golf on a Friday morning at the expense of all the other things I can be doing in pastoral ministry, writing, or family life (which are endless), I had better be doing so knowing that this is where God wants me. Just because it's my day off does not mean that I am free from obedience; yet sometimes golfing is exactly where God wants me.

2. *"Take up your cross."* The cross is persecution, rejection, and pain resulting from obedience to God in a world hostile to his desires. As Christ endured these for us, so we will risk them for him. We will often be forced to choose between pleasing the world or pleasing God. If you choose against the world, it will make you pay. Prepare for it. Every obedience will not end in temporal bliss. We are called to "fellowship in his suffering" as well as to share his power.

Such fellowship, however, is not a cause for despair. Whatever you sacrifice in this life is nothing compared to the value of knowing Christ more fully. Only those who have loved God through painful experiences know the depth of joy it can bring. Though the search for pleasure will never lead to God's will, there is no pleasure greater than that which flows from God's presence to his obedient child. Even the temporal joys of this life are multiplied when they are an expression of our obedience to him.

3. *"Follow me."* Even though the flesh screams, we are free to ignore it and follow Christ. That is as simple as it sounds, and a source of great peace. My pursuit of God often puts me in situations far beyond my knowledge or experience. I've prayed for sicknesses that only got worse, and tried to help desperate people whom psychiatrists had already given up on. That can easily lead to anxiety. What am I going to do? How can I make a difference?

Then I remember this simple instruction: "Follow me." I don't have to come up with the solution. It doesn't hang on me. I'm just a disciple with a simple agenda—follow the Master wherever he goes. If I don't know what to do, I can only tell people that I'll seek God with them until he gives us an answer.

We destroy expediency not by trying to be sinless or by assaulting our flesh but only by being preoccupied with pleasing Jesus. As we continue to draw close to him despite the objections of our flesh, it will have to die. Then we are free to obey God without trying to save ourselves.

This is the drive that motivates God's people. We see it in Daniel when his enemies threatened to throw him to the lions if he persisted in praying openly to God. How easily he could have justified less-conspicuous prayers so as not to alienate his peers! But he didn't, and God was glorified in his obedience.

Consider Timothy. After the church had already passed a resolution saying that circumcision was not essential to salvation, he offered himself to be circumcised. He could have defended his freedom in the name of not giving in to those who were being legalistic with the gospel. Instead he gave up his freedom to help the legalists see its power.

Our bent for personal expedience can also be overcome as we seek to please only Jesus with our lives. After he gave up so much to save us, what else would we want to do?

A Life of Accountability

No matter what situation I face, I know that three things are true: 1) God has a will in it; 2) he wants me to know what that will is; and 3) he wants to give me the strength to obey it.

Living by these three truths helps me to keep focused on God's desires for my life, but it isn't always easy. Sometimes I plow through a situation, either forgetting to seek his will or confident that my own wisdom would line up with his if I did. Other times I resist making a firm conclusion on what I believe God wants me to do because I'm not sure of what it is or because I have an inkling that his preference will not be mine. Even when I get through all of that and can affirm his will, if I don't rely on *his* strength I find my own insufficient against the weakness of my flesh.

Unless we hold ourselves accountable, our intentions to please God will not be realized. The two most important areas for accountability come in knowing God's will and obeying it.

"But how can I be sure what God is saying to me?" I'm asked that question more than any other in counseling, and it is a good one. Even though I've made it clear that God wants to communicate with us and gave a list of ways in which he does that, the process is not exact. Even though God's gifts are perfect, Paul says that we are not able to respond to them perfectly. The result is that "we know in part and we prophesy in part," just as if we were looking at "a poor reflection" as in a mirror (1 Corinthians 13:9-12).

Our intimacy will be perfect only when we meet him face-to-face. Now we only perceive bits and pieces of God's mind, not ever seeing the whole picture. We cannot trust our methods of hearing him to be completely accurate. Even our flesh will try to pass off its own desires as God's voice. But this doesn't mean that we can't be sure. Our perception of God's will can be tested by two external sources. One is absolute and the other is just a helpful addition to the process.

First, anything we think that God has said to us must stand up to the revelation of God in the Scriptures.

> All Scripture is God-breathed and is useful for teaching, rebuking, correcting and training in righteousness, so that the man of God may be thoroughly equipped for every good work (2 Timothy 3:16,17).

Anything that does not align with the content and spirit of God's Word must be abandoned without question. I can't tell you the number of times I've prayed over a situation and then felt like God gave me some insight to deal with it, only to find that exact thing specifically addressed in the Word as I turned to my Bible reading for the day.

One morning I had prayed about some miscommunications in the church office where I worked that had left me hurt and wounded. As I prayed about this I determined not to waste another day trying to cooperate. I would just get my own work done and ignore everyone else. That resolved, I opened to my Bible reading for the day. The first verse I saw was, "He who separates himself seeks his own desire; he quarrels against all sound wisdom" (Proverbs 18:1 NASB). Needless to say, I abandoned my course and that day saw God heal relationships that were important to me.

Specific texts like that are helpful, but we also need to look at a wider perspective. Can we imagine Jesus doing what we're about to do? How quickly such thinking exposes our own desires! That kind of perspective demands a familiarity with the Word gained only by regular feeding from it.

> The word of God is living and active. Sharper than any double-edged sword. . .it judges the thoughts and attitudes of the heart (Hebrews 4:12).

There is no valid intimacy with God apart from the full application of his Word. This is the objective test that keeps intimacy from being a figment of our imagination. Hearing God's voice doesn't lessen our need for Scripture, but rather heightens it.

The Joy of Mutual Submission

The second source of confirmation is other believers. People who consider themselves accountable to God's truth will humbly seek the input of others. So much abuse is perpetrated at this level that it is difficult to write about and hope to be heard, but Scripture encourages us to admonish one another and to submit to each other.

In the last five years I've made no significant decisions without the prayer and counsel of other believers. I share with them what I sense is God's leading and seek their honest comments. They test my perspectives with their own and with the Word. I've come to respect that process. They don't make decisions for me, but they help me meet my responsibility to follow God.

I make sure that those I share with are walking in close relationship with God. I'm not looking for worldly wisdom here, but people to help me affirm God's direction. In the context of mutual submission I've rarely had to make a decision that we weren't agreed on at the end. When we haven't found that agreement even after much sharing and prayer, I still follow the conviction of my heart, though with great caution. Mutual submission calls us to genuine openness to each other, but not to violate our conscience if the process doesn't bring unity.

Coming to unity, however, is always the goal. Philippians describes that process:

> If you have any encouragement from being united with Christ, if any comfort from his love, if any fellowship with the Spirit, if any tenderness and compassion, then make my joy complete by being like-minded, having the same love, being one in spirit and purpose. Do nothing out of selfish ambition or vain conceit, but in humility consider others better than yourselves (Philippians 2:1-3).

Mutual submission demands unity in Christ, deep love and tenderness that puts the needs of others on a par with our own, and sensitivity to the Spirit. Building these into relationships is a key priority of body life. Where such a lifestyle exists, Paul says we can trust the process of unity. Here we can share our insights and seek God until we can affirm his voice together.

People are continually amazed at the relationship I have with my copastor, Mark Condie, and frankly so am I. We've been together for seven years sharing the work of ministry and are still good friends. "Now come on, isn't one of you really over the other?" they ask. I can't blame them; copastoring has a poor track record in this century. In the early church, however, it wasn't so. They were always ministering in teams of at least two, and one has to force his interpretation on the text to conclude that one was superior to the others.

Our copastoring works not because of a hidden order, special chemistry, or sovereign act of God. It works because we both understand our accountability before God to do his will in this congregation. Jesus is our Senior Pastor. We are both on his staff. Our task is not to balance what Wayne wants with what Mark wants, but to find out what God wants. Each of us has different pieces of the puzzle that God is putting together. So we listen to each other and pray together, cooperating until we come to agreement. Then we can move with confidence that we've heard God. It has worked for us and the numerous teams that share leadership in our body.

The body of Christ also offers another form of accountability. Once we know the will of God, we can let other believers check up on us to make sure we're following through. How easy it is to let our obedience slide if we're not faced with a tangible moment of accountability! If you're having trouble being in the Word every day, ask another believer who is praying for you and checking on you every couple of days to see if you're doing it. You'll find that it will really help.

Helping each other in this way can be easily abused if we don't keep one thing in mind: When I'm helping someone be accountable, I am only helping him in areas where he knows that God is dealing with him. If I impose my own standards of righteousness on other people I will harm their growth.

Learning to recognize God's voice and obey it is a process of trial and error. If God has spoken, your obedience will confirm it. I've stepped out in areas, certain that I had heard from God. My actions didn't violate the Word and other people confirmed them, but in the doing I found out that they weren't from God. By hindsight I almost always see how God was trying to stop me, but also how I pushed ahead because I wanted my own way so badly. Failures can be great tools to learning if we're humble enough to admit them and adjust accordingly. God is also bigger than our failures and can even use them to our good when our hearts are seeking him.

A Pattern for Supportive Leadership

I began these two chapters on restoring personal responsibility by showing how current models of leadership are ineffective in promoting it. Now I think you can see why.

We use Old Testament forms of leadership that were not designed for the glory of the new covenant. Moses' dominating leadership with its delegation of authority through elders is often referred to as God's pattern for the church today. That is regrettable, since all the ground rules have changed since the time of Moses.

Prior to the coming of the Holy Spirit, God dealt with a society by dealing with its leader, whether king, prophet, or priest. People would follow God by following his anointed one, but that wasn't ideal. As Moses laid hands on his 70 elders to convey his anointing on them, two other men began to prophesy in the camp. Joshua encouraged Moses to stop them, but he responded, "I wish that all God's people were prophets and that the Lord would put his Spirit on them!" (Numbers 11:29). He looked forward to a better day.

So did the prophet Joel. "I will pour out my Spirit on all people. Your sons and daughters will prophesy. . . . Even on my servants, both men and women, I will pour out my Spirit in those days" (Joel 2:28,29). Moses' dream was affirmed. One day all of God's people would hear his voice.

On the day of Pentecost Peter pronounced this outpouring as the fulfillment of God's promise. People would no longer have to rely on leaders telling them what God wants; they could know him themselves. The early church never exemplified the leadership-dependence of the Old Testament. They did have leaders to help affirm God's working and to equip believers, but they didn't dominate the ministry of the body.

> The New Testament simply does not speak in terms of two classes of Christians—"ministers" and "laymen" as we do today. According to the Bible, the people of God comprise all Christians, and all Christians through the exercise of spiritual gifts have some "work of ministry." . . . The clergy-laity dichotomy is unbiblical and therefore invalid. It grew up as an accident of church history and actually marked a drift away from biblical faithfulness.[1]

The alternative to kings in the body of Christ is not anarchy. For everyone to do "what is right in their own eyes" leads to as much destruction as those who lord it over others. The nature of life in the body of Christ must ensure that Jesus Christ is personally at the helm. That can only happen where each person takes responsibility for pursuing his will and works that out in mutual submission to others.

God gives leadership to his body not to be a substitute for his presence, but to equip the body and coordinate its ministry so that those who seek their own will cannot dominate its affairs. Scripture gives us two keys of such leadership.

1. *Leaders must be mature followers of Jesus.* The body is not a democracy in which everyone on the spectrum between carnal and perfect has an equal voice. First Timothy 3 lists the requirements for leadership, and all have to do with personal integrity and spiritual maturity.

Unfortunately, church leadership is regarded more as a profession that one prepares for academically than as a role necessitating personal maturity. David Watson struggled with this same problem: "Most of the mainline churches place too great an emphasis on academic training and too little on spiritual renewal and life."[2] Even unpaid leaders in churches are too often chosen because they're rich, have a good business sense, or are popular, and not because they are sensitive to God.

2. *Leadership must be plural.* Every example of leadership in the New Testament is shared among teams of mature believers. Shared leadership allows the body to be coordinated without being manipulated, since people are not projected into Jesus' role. Furthermore, the confirmation of others is a necessary part of discovering God's will, since we all see only in part.

Leaders are not people who stand above the body with any special relationship with God. Though they have specific functions in helping to equip the flock, they can only be successful as a fellow struggler on the way to wholeness. The essence of pastoring is to help sheep by standing beside them, as much involved in the struggles of life as they are. These incisive words from Frederick Buechner sum it up:

> He is called not to be an actor, a magician, in the pulpit. He is called to be himself. He is called to tell the truth as he has experienced it. He is called to be human and that is calling enough for any man. If he does not make real to them the human experience of what it is to cry in the storm and receive no answer, to be sick at heart and find no healing, then he becomes the only one there who seems not to have had the experience, because most surely under the bonnets and shawls and jackets, under the Afros and ponytails, all the others there have had it whether they talk of it or not.[3]

God hungers for that kind of leadership. Only in that context can people come into the fullness of intimacy with God and be used by God to touch others. Church leaders must ensure that they are supporting this process and not supplanting it.

Beware the Spirit
of the Age

13
Confessions of a Christian Materialist

THE LOSS OF PERSPECTIVE

*What is highly valued among men
is detestable in God's sight.*
—Luke 16:15

The weeklong pastor's seminar included the opportunity to join our host congregation for their Wednesday evening service. During the time they usually set aside to intercede for the nations of the world, the pastor shared a vision he had of dark clouds of judgment hanging ominously over America. The only thing that could push back the cloud was the fervent prayers of God's people. What had been a casual time of prayer up until that moment suddenly grew intense. I joined in too. If there's anything I take pains to avoid, it's pain.

That was still on my mind the next morning as I finished my prayer time and turned to read the Word. My reading for the day was Psalm 98. I was in for quite a shock.

> Let the sea resound, and everything in it, the world, and all who live in it. Let the rivers clap their hands, let the mountains sing together for joy; Let them sing before the Lord, for he comes to judge the earth.

As I often do when reading the Psalms, I was using the psalmist's words to express worship to God. I was flowing along with the rivers and the mountains, clapping and singing until that last phrase jarred me to a stop. I don't know if I had ever really taken note before of what had launched creation into such ecstasy. It was God's judgment! Why was creation worshiping so excitedly over the very thing I was praying so hard to prevent?

145

Why didn't I want God to judge America? Doesn't judgment force people to see the emptiness of life without God? Doesn't it end the deceptions that men hold over one another, rewarding the truly righteous and exposing those who have only pretended to be so? Doesn't it restore justice and freedom for the oppressed and invite people to return to God?

Of course I wanted all of those things, but I feared what it might take to bring them to pass. If God's judgment took the form of an economic depression, my money would become worthless like everyone else's, and I would risk having to cope with scarcity. If he judged us by the invasion of a wicked foreign power, I too would lose my freedom. And if a plague swept us I would be involved with people tormented by it.

I was face-to-face with the truth. My priorities were vested in the material world as much as people around me who did not love God. Theologically I valued my walk with Jesus more than any other possession I had, but the others rated such a close second that I doubt anyone could have told the difference. God's primary blessings to me were material, and I didn't want him to do anything that would put those at risk.

I had become a Christian materialist, if such people exist—though I don't think they do except in someone's mind. In reality, the materialist part always devours the Christian part.

The Myths of Stewardship

Since that day I've reevaluated a number of major Christian tenets. I know I risk sounding heretical here because in this culture we have married materialism to Christianity. We have even given its offspring a biblical name—stewardship—and under its protection we pursue material security, prosperity, and comfort, thinking these to be only an extension of our obedience to God.

As I've looked closely I've found four concepts which are readily accepted in Christendom today but which are actually nothing more than myths.

1. *The abundant life and the American dream are the same thing.* We have erroneously assumed that God wants his followers to

have two cars in their suburban garages, employment with a great future, and the adoration of everyone around them. I once knew a man who served the outcasts of our society with the love of Jesus. He could pack everything he owned into the back of a Toyota, yet strangely he seemed happier than most people with far more. He didn't even act like he was making any big sacrifice. Maybe he wasn't.

When Jesus uttered the words that head this chapter, "What is highly valued among men is detestable in God's sight," he wasn't talking about immorality or secular humanism. He was talking about preoccupation with temporal possessions. The abundant life is something far more wonderful than money could ever buy.

2. *Riches are the gift of God.* Whenever someone gets a raise, a better job, or an unexpected windfall, God always gets the credit. Conversely, whenever someone has a major unexpected expense or his business suffers a downturn, we blame that on the devil. That's strange given the fact that I've rarely seen increased riches draw anyone closer to God, but I've seen them draw many people away. People get so busy enjoying what their newfound money can buy that they suddenly find they have no time or energy to pursue God with all their heart.

Francis of Assisi was born into one of the richest homes in his Italian village. Francis' obedience to God, however, put him at odds with his parents' expectations, so they set out to disinherit him. Standing before the town tribunal, his father demanded back from his son everything he had received from the family wealth. Francis stripped himself to only a single undergarment and handed it along with all his money to his father. "Hereafter I shall not say Father Petro di Bernardone, but Our Father who art in heaven."[1] He went on to teach the church the joy and beauty of being free from the chains of materialism—a lesson it quickly forgot.

When I first read this story as a Christian materialist I was horrified at Francis' lack of tact. If he hadn't offended his parents, imagine how God could have used all that money to make his ministry even greater! But God knew that the price of this wealth was too high. The concessions necessary to keep it would have destroyed the ministry it was supposed to have helped. I suspect the same was at stake when Jesus dealt with the rich young ruler, telling him to give away everything he had. Jesus wasn't testing his commitment but was telling him the money he loved was keeping him from the life of Jesus that he wanted.

3. *It takes money to minister.* This is drilled into our heads weekly, by media ministries and by those little speeches that precede the church offering. If the only way the church can touch the world is through TV shows and fancy buildings, then maybe the propaganda is right. But God doesn't limit himself to how much money his people have. He led more than six million people out of Egypt and sustained them in the wilderness for more than 40 years without so much as an offering. They never had a gross national product, but their needs were met.

There is no recorded incident of Jesus soliciting money from anyone, though he did get some from a fish once. We know of some women who helped him with personal support, but he didn't spend anything on ministry. He never rented an auditorium or built a building. When he dealt with the money problems of the rich young ruler he asked him to give his money to the poor, not the JC Evangelistic Association.

Can you imagine an evangelist who could write a letter that didn't appeal for money? Most of Paul's letters didn't, and the ones that did were to help starving believers in Jerusalem. This is not to say that money can't be used for ministry. The early church often paid those who served full-time and sent out evangelists by underwriting their expenses. The point is that no one equated ministry with money. They ministered the life of Jesus with or without it, understanding that the basis of effective ministry demands something more than money—people!

If I had the choice of filling a city with 100 people who carry the power and love of God with them into every situation they encountered for a week, or else sponsoring an hour-long sermon by a TV evangelist, I have no doubt which would have greater impact. And the people needn't cost a dime to send out. The church today links money with ministry not because it is more effective but because it is easier to get.

4. *God's first priority for my life is material.* We may be theologically committed to the idea that our spiritual nature is more important than our material circumstances, but why do we seek God more intensely for physical healings than we do freedom from our sins? Why do our prayers have more to do with God changing our circumstances to bring peace into our lives than with God changing *us* so that our circumstances don't affect us so deeply?

Where have you directed the majority of your effort this week—to physical comfort or to spiritual maturity? I'm not saying that God is unconcerned with the material elements of our life, but that they are not his *primary* concern. When we make them our primary concern we will always be frustrated because God is not living up to our expectations. Instead he is only inviting us to live at a level of fulfillment far beyond them.

The Materialistic Invasion

There's a difference between adapting the gospel to the terms of our generation and accommodating the gospel to meet our generation's terms. Our approach to materialism has done the latter.

The quest for material comfort is a basic drive of humanity. It usually begins by trying to acquire the basic necessities to survive—food, a place to live, and acceptance by other people. Once those are secured, however, our hunger for sustenance quickly becomes a lust for luxury. Having enough is replaced by the desire to have more and better possessions.

Instead of challenging this materialistic drive, people today are equating God's blessing with material happiness and success. The prosperity movement leads the way in bribing people into a relationship with God. "There is no question that God wants us to be financially prosperous"[2] is how one faith teacher puts it.

Dave Wilkerson points out the error in such thinking: "The prosperity message works in a time of prosperity. Good times, fine message. It soothes our conscience, it soothes our covetous spirits, it gives us an excuse to live high. Is this the church Christ is coming for, with a Cadillac theology?"[3]

For many today stewardship is nothing more than greed in sheep's clothing, allowing people to pursue their materialistic bent and cloaking it in religious terminology. As Richard Foster says in *Celebration of Discipline,* "Covetousness we call ambition. Hoarding we call prudence. Greed we call industry."[4]

One fund-raiser for a major TV evangelist explained to me the organization's basis for motivating people: "We know more people will give money out of greed than a pure heart, and we don't mind appealing to greed to get it." This results in a gospel that appeals to the flesh, where people think God's favor can be purchased with their offerings.

People who try such giving will always be disappointed with God when he does not meet their expectations. Paul warned us against false teachers "who think that godliness is a means to financial gain." He continued, "People who want to get rich fall into temptation and a trap and into many foolish and harmful desires that plunge men into ruin and destruction."

Our preoccupation with the material goes far beyond money. Christian bookstores are filled with books proclaiming how the work of Jesus promises maximum sexual fulfillment, an easier way to a slimmer you, quick success, self-acceptance, and freedom from emotional stress. "One general principle that publishers recognize is that Christians are interested in the same topics that interest non-Christians. This is not to say that Christian readers are 'worldly minded,' but rather that the same issues of life affect all humans."[5]

The conclusion is so obvious that it has to be denied in the telling. What sells today appeals to the materialistic mindset of believers, while challenging books on discipleship and self-denial largely go unread or unheeded.

The problem here is preoccupation and priority. Are we serving Jesus in order to be changed into his image or to extend our quest for material comfort? I do not want to suggest that God does not care about the material aspects of our life, our sexual fulfillment, or our personal health. He does—but he also knows how easily our preoccupation with those things can destroy our love for himself.

We can also run to the opposite extreme and condemn the material elements of this world as inherently evil. Poverty is no more a virtue than prosperity. I said earlier that many inspiring believers were poor, but some were also rich. Mary and Martha seemed to be, and Jesus didn't condemn them for it. Being preoccupied with material simplicity can also distract us from God, since its focus is still on material things.

Life in Christ challenges us to only one priority: the vitality of our spiritual life in Christ over the comforts of this age. Recently, when asked how the church has failed before the world, Malcolm Muggeridge responded, "I would say only by this readiness to accept the materialist's basis of the Christian faith. And once you do that the game is up."[6]

Being material creatures in a material world is obviously more apparent to us than our also being spiritual creatures in a spiritual world, but more obvious isn't more important. The challenge of intimacy is to come to grips with the fact that we live with these two natures where these two worlds intersect. We cannot deny the material, for God doesn't. But it cannot be our basis for living.

Spiritual People in a Material World

In the area of materialism it is always easier to criticize others than look at ourselves. If we hunger for intimacy, however, we cannot afford to be smug about this issue, since we are all within its grasp. Who doesn't see someone get a new car or home and twinge with a desire to have the same? Who doesn't want a more fulfilling job, hopefully with more pay and vacation time?

The drive for material happiness provides the arena for the continuing battle between the flesh and the spirit. Will we give in to it, or find freedom from it? James 4 talks about the depth of this drive and the destruction it causes:

> When you ask you do not receive, because you ask with wrong motives, that you may spend what you get on your

> pleasures. . . . Anyone who chooses to be a friend of the
> world becomes an enemy of God. Or do you think Scrip-
> ture says without reason that the spirit he caused to live in
> us tends toward envy, but he gives us more grace?

The mark of our fallen nature is intense envy, which craves
material comfort and happiness. We see things we don't have
and waste a lot of effort devising ways to get them. This
preoccupation has its greatest impact on our relationship
with God.

The subtitle of this chapter is "The Loss of Perspective,"
and that is the real danger of our materialistic drives. People
who would rather pursue the world's goods than God's life
represent only one aspect of the problem. Materialism also
distorts the perspective of those who want to walk with God,
and it does so by setting their concerns primarily on externals.

As long as we're only concerned with our own well-being,
we will miss God's working in our lives. His greatest concerns
are not material but spiritual. He is concerned with the transformation of our lives and the extension of his love to those
who don't know him. Those objectives are rarely fulfilled in
this age through personal comfort. Even a cursory reading
of Hebrews 11 will show you that most of the acts which faith
called people to led them initially into circumstances of greater
hardship.

That's why Jesus warned the Pharisees, "Stop judging by
mere appearances, and make a right judgment" (John 7:24).
Their preoccupation with externals kept them from seeing
things through God's eyes. The same thing will ally us with
the world against God, and it explains how vital Christianity is
daily traded away for gold and silver. To gain the world's
goods you have to play the world's game.

Our attempts to merge materialism with Christianity only
result in making God a vehicle for our wants rather than
ourselves a vessel for his will. Once we do this we forfeit God's
life. "It is time to awaken to the fact that conformity to a sick
society is to be sick. Until we see how unbalanced our culture

has become at this point we will not be able to deal with the mammon spirit within ourselves nor will we desire Christian simplicity."[7]

God will not cater to our envy, and James makes it clear that our attempts to get him to do so will only result in unanswered prayer. How many people have become frustrated with God because they were promised he would fulfill their materialistic desires? Instead of learning to turn from their selfish desires, they turned from him convinced of his powerlessness.

When the world looks in on today's church it finds it every bit as preoccupied with the good life as the world is, and with just as much success. Though this might appeal to some people, it alienates far more. Those who are hungry are looking for something better than the rat race that plagues them.

And this "something better" is exactly what James promised us: "God gives us more grace"—not to meet our material desires but to free us from them so we can participate in his glory.

Something Greater Than Material Comfort

God's work in us doesn't renounce materialism as evil—just insignificant compared to his splendor. He has offered us heavenly treasures that are not only far more valuable than the wealth of our surroundings and the health of our bodies but also indestructible and unstealable (Matthew 6:20).

James Dobson tells of skillfully slaughtering his family one evening in Monopoly, only to be left to put up the game by himself. As he did, God showed him how much this experience was a parable on the material things we gain in this life. No matter what we gain in this life, at the end it will all go back in the box.[8]

God offers us his glory, a possession that will not go back in the box when it's all over. The materialism of this age need not keep us from his glory if we understand what Jesus told us about our material needs and desires in this age:

> Do not worry, saying, "What shall we eat?" or "What shall we drink?" or "What shall we wear?" For the pagans

run after all these things, and your heavenly Father
knows that you need them. But seek first his kingdom
and his righteousness, and all these things will be given
to you as well (Matthew 6:31-33).

God wants to free us from every material ambition, entrusting their fulfillment to him. He knows what we need and what
we can enjoy without having it destroy us. If we will just be
preoccupied with knowing him and seeking to be conformed
to the image of Jesus, he will supply everything we need—
physical, emotional, and spiritual—out of his abundant goodness.

This does not mean that we should sit around all day and
read the Bible, assuming that God will take care of us. Paul
sharply warned some who tried this in Thessalonica that if
they wouldn't work they also shouldn't eat. Obedience to God
will lead us to meet our responsibilities in this life with greater
diligence than a lust for possessions could ever produce.

Practically, this approach to our material needs means that
we give all of our possessions and desires to God. When God
owns them, able to freely use them as he sees fit, they can't own
us. Look for ways to use the resources God has given you to
extend his kingdom. Don't make decisions about any major
purchase without seeking God's instructions, being careful
not to overextend yourself by buying things you can't afford.

The path of intimacy is neither wealth nor poverty. It is
obedience to God, completely apart from the material ramifications of doing so. This perspective will lead to a true
enjoyment of the things he gives us, and true contentment
even in the face of things we lack.

Anyone who has ever tasted of God's presence, or the joy of
being obedient to him even when it cost something, knows
that nothing material can offer greater joy. If you don't know
that, then the greatest joy available to you in this life is still
ahead of you.

14

The Righteousness That Comes from Faith

I delight greatly in the Lord;
my soul rejoices in my God.
For he has clothed me
with garments of salvation
and arrayed me in a robe of righteousness.
—Isaiah 61:10

Righteousness.

No other word connected with the life of God breeds less excitement than this one. Terms such as intimacy, peace, abundant life, healing, joy, and wholeness all evoke hunger. We relish these gifts of God—but righteousness? People turn up their noses the moment they hear the word, and that is truly sad, for righteousness is the greatest gift that God has offered us.

The enemy has so disfigured people's concept of holiness that many no longer recognize it, much less want it, in their lives. Many see it as an unreasonable list of rules they must obey, while others see it as demands they are incapable of satisfying. Both are a far cry from the righteousness that Jesus wants to give us. At best many people see righteousness as one of the unpleasant costs of being a Christian or as a way to gain God's favor.

Peter said that nothing could be further from the truth: "[God] sent [Jesus] first to you to bless you by turning each of you from your wicked ways" (Acts 3:26). Our freedom from sin is not a necessary pain to get God's blessing, but that freedom itself is God's blessing.

Righteousness is God entrusting his glory to earthen vessels. It is liberation from the destructive forces that rip our lives apart and estrange us from fellowship with God. Seeking that instead of material comfort will restore the perspective we need to see God and walk with Him.

A Hunger for Holiness

Paul's words in Philippians 3:7-11 have been affectionately called the Magnificent Obsession. Paul talks about the drive that directed the course of his life: "I consider everything a loss compared to the surpassing greatness of knowing Christ Jesus my Lord." Paul wanted to grow closer to Jesus with every passing day.

Just *knowing* Christ, however, wasn't the only thing for which Paul hungered. He also wanted to be *like* him: "I consider [all things] rubbish that I may gain Christ and be found in him, not having a righteousness of my own that comes from law, but that which is through faith in Christ." Paul didn't see righteousness as competing with his pleasure; it *was* his pleasure.

But Paul made it clear that the righteousness he sought was not one which comes by observing law. He knew that kind of righteousness all too well. Just a few verses before he talked about his life as a Pharisee: "As for legalistic righteousness, [I was] faultless." Before he came to know Jesus, Paul knew the bondage of trying to please God by a system of rules and regulations. He knew its frustration and rigidity, and how miserable he was in his own success. He repudiated this system and clearly distinguished it from the righteousness that comes by faith.

The major reason believers don't hunger for holiness today is because they misunderstand the process that brings it to them. Despite Jesus' work on the cross and his implementation of a new Covenant that promised to change us from the inside out, the approach of Western Christianity to righteousness is not much different from that of the Pharisees. Though we admit that Christ fulfilled the law on our behalf, and mock all the picky rules the Pharisees had made up to make God's law to Moses more clear, we nonetheless have continued their tradition.

Today we call them "New Testament principles" and in some places even "God's laws." Our lists are just as long and our rules just as picky. Look at our prescribed guidelines today for worship services, marriages, dating, finances, and successful church programs. When God's presence loses reality among his people they always retreat to codes of conduct.

God's Word does give us clear instructions about what pleases him, but we make a fatal step when we encourage people to fulfill those instructions outside the context of their own vibrant relationship with God. Pathetically, legalistic righteousness is the only kind most people know about, even though it is always destined for failure.

Richard Foster, summing up a study of the book of Romans, made this conclusion:

> The apostle Paul went to great lengths to show that righteousness is a gift of God. He used the term thirty-five times in that epistle and each time struck home the fact that righteousness is unattained and unattainable through human effort.[1]

Attempting to gain righteousness through human achievement can yield only two results, both negative. First, the strong of will can produce an external righteousness, but it is only skin deep. Jesus pointed past the righteousness of the Pharisees to the greed, hate, and pride that seethed beneath the surface. Such people retreat to a false security that insulates them from God's presence.

Second, and most common, is the frustration which many people feel when that method keeps failing. When I was younger I remember being overrun with conviction, confessing my sin to God, and promising never to succumb again. But it never worked, and every few months I was back there again trying to convince God I was serious. I felt so deeply condemned because I thought if I really loved God enough I could choose him above my sin.

Without a proper understanding of how we participate in God's righteousness we are prevented from fully tasting God's goodness. Nothing pales the temporal happiness that sin offers any faster than the joy of God's presence. Many people have never seen a Christianity that exciting and vibrant. All they've seen is people weighted down by the obligations of church attendance, Christian works, and ethics.

No wonder people are not excited about God's righteousness—they've never found a way to participate in it! But Paul spoke of a righteousness that comes from faith, one that is produced in us as we simply love God. I know this sounds too good to be true, but doesn't everything else about God sound that way too?

The remainder of this chapter will show how God makes us righteous so that we can cooperate with him and reap the fruits of it. Before we look closely at the process, however, there is one prerequisite: To be free of our sin we need to view it like God does. This is the heart of repentance, an attitude we must continue to cultivate as we walk with God.

Our struggle with sin does not end just because we become believers. No matter how successful we are at hiding it for a time, eventually we come face-to-face with our own sin. We reap its consequences and know how much we grieve God. And since few people confess sins to others anymore, we feel alone in our struggle, the bad apple that can't get it right.

But guilt alone won't bring us to freedom. Even Scripture states that sin is pleasurable at least for a time (Hebrews 11:25), and explains how it easily entices us to do the very thing we don't want to do (Romans 7:18-20). To see our sin as God does, we must see the destruction that it causes us. As long as we think of it only as God's test to see if we love him more than having fun, we miss the point.

Sin doesn't hurt him, it hurts us—and only him because of what it does to us. We've been told that sin separates God from us because he cannot look on it, but who hid from whom in the Garden of Eden! It wasn't God in the bushes, but Adam and Eve. God can and does come to us in our sin, but our sin makes us cringe from his presence and blinds us to his reality.

His warnings about sin are not to see if we love pleasure more than him, but to tell us that sin destroys us. God denies it to us for the same reason we deny our children the freedom of playing with a can of gasoline and a book of matches. When we see sin in this light, no one could ever truly love God without hating sin as well.

The church continues to miscommunicate this fact in its passion to condemn sin. We think the fear of judgment will bring repentance so we rail at people for not adhering to God's standards. We say we hate the sin but love the sinner, but never find a way to live that out well enough to convey it by our actions. We end up either looking like we love both or hate both.

Jerry Cook, author of *Love, Acceptance and Forgiveness*, demonstrated in an interview with *Leadership* magazine how the two can fit together:

> I remember the first homosexual I ever talked to at length. I realized two things: (1) I really cared for him and (2) I was deeply committed to the fact that his lifestyle would utterly destroy him. Now—how to convey both of those facts? I said to him at one point, "I am really committed to you as a person. I love you, and in doing so am committed to confronting your lifestyle and helping you see how destructive it is."[2]

Such a view of sin gives way to hunger. Righteousness is not our punishment; it is our joy. Those who earnestly seek the righteousness of God and find it will never be miserable, but full of joy. This is the righteousness that comes from faith. To see how God brings it into our lives, let's first see how sin works in us.

The Way of Sin

No one had to teach us how to sin. The desire to please ourselves leads to sin quite naturally. You can even see it in children only a few months old. They want what they want when they want it and are willing to make anyone around them miserable until they get it. Crying to make a need known develops quickly into a demand to get it *now*.

James 1:14,15 tells us how sin works in us:

> Each one is tempted when, by his own evil desire, he is dragged away and enticed. Then, after desire has conceived, it gives birth to sin; and sin, when it is full-grown, gives birth to death.

Though we often blame it on the devil, the enticement to sin comes from within us. We all have desires centered on self-pleasure. When that desire meets an opportunity to fulfill it, sin is conceived.

Living by the quest for material comfort will make every circumstance a temptation. The enemy helps the process by creating circumstances that will focus us on our sins and give us the opportunity to fulfill them. James compares this meeting of desire and opportunity to a sperm and an egg. When they come together, sin is born. He continues the analogy by saying that matured sin results in death.

The death referred to here is not just our physical death, but also the death of our spiritual nature. This process of death starts with our very first sin, slowly destroying us from the inside.

Notice that what is important in this process is not the acts we call sin, but the evil desires that produced them. Sin is measured by our motives, not our actions. The Pharisees even made fasting and prayer a sinful act because they did it for the praise of men and not the love of God.

To find out how Jesus sets us free from sin, let's consider four different views about how we should deal with our sin.

1. Many people want Jesus to break the chain only at the last link. As fallen creatures we will always sin; we just don't want to bear the consequences of it. Salvation can't heal us from sin; it just ensures that it won't result in our eternal death.

Dietrich Bonhoeffer called this message cheap grace because it is so incomplete. It doesn't challenge us to change, but just provides us with an excuse. Who could ever content himself with forgiveness that can't bring healing? If we really hate our sin, we will want to be free of it.

2. Others think we're just not supposed to sin. People who believe this try to conquer sin by sheer force of will. They have strong desires to sin, and even the opportunities to do so, but they think they should receive enough grace from Jesus not to sin. This is the legalistic righteousness we spoke of earlier and James doesn't give this idea much credibility. Once desire and opportunity conceive, he said, sin is born.

You might be able to hold off an evil desire for a time, but eventually it will wear you down. The denial of fulfillment only increases the desire. The only way to win by this means is to redefine sin so as to only include those things you are not tempted to do or can fulfill for other selfish motives, as the Pharisees did.

3. Another option would be to not allow our desires to have the opportunity of fulfillment. This sounds good and probably gave rise to the monastic movement. It assumes that righteousness can be achieved by creating a vacuum where no temptation exists. Throw out your TV; avoid unsaved friends; don't put yourself in any situation where you can fall to sin.

Though this thinking has some merit, it too is incomplete. Certainly we shouldn't toy with those things that destroy us. Someone dealing with lust shouldn't have a stack of *Playboy* under his bed. But we cannot rid ourselves of all temptation, and even if we did, this would only result in frustration because our intense desires would go unfulfilled and unhealed. This solution also focuses only on negative acts and doesn't prepare us to live in obedience that extends Christ's life to other people. Obedience omitted is sin as well.

4. That leaves only one other place to deal with our sin: our self-based desires. And that is exactly where Jesus pointed in Matthew 5: "You have heard that it was said . . . 'Do not murder.' . . . But I tell you that anyone who is angry with his brother will be subject to judgment."

I used to hate this passage. I grew up in the church, never committing the "serious" sins the Bible deals with, and this passage made me feel like just when I got things right God changed the ground rules. I had been denying myself desires that others were fulfilling. Why should I bear the same punishment as those who had the pleasure of doing them?

What a warped view we have of sin! Jesus was not attempting to increase our guilt with this passage but to identify where he wants to heal us. Sin begins in the self-awareness that produces our evil thoughts. God wants to turn the process around and make righteousness flow as easily out of my life as sin used to.

The Way of Righteousness

In Romans 6:12-23 Paul outlines the process of righteousness that can be produced in us by faith. It stands as an excellent counterpoint to the Scripture we just examined in James. Here are a few excerpts:

> Count yourselves dead to sin but alive to God in Christ Jesus. Therefore do not let sin reign in your mortal body so that you obey its evil desires. Do not offer the parts of your body to sin, as instruments of wickedness, but rather offer yourselves to God . . . and offer the parts of your body to him as instruments of righteousness.
>
> Don't you know that when you offer yourselves to someone to obey him as slaves, you are slaves to the one whom you obey—whether you are slaves to sin, which leads to death, or to obedience, which leads to righteousness?
>
> But now that you have been set free from sin and have become slaves to God, the benefit you reap is holiness, and the result is eternal life. For the wages of sin is death, but the gift of God is eternal life in Christ Jesus our Lord.

By using Paul's instruction we can clearly see how God wants to make us righteous.

Righteousness begins within us. Even as the evil desires within us met opportunity and produced sin, so God's desires within us can find opportunity to bear righteousness. Instead of every circumstance being a temptation, it becomes a legitimate trial to use my faith to obey God. As I live in that faith, with my heart oriented on pleasing God, holiness results. When that holiness matures, it yields the fruit of eternal life.

This is not to say that righteousness earns eternal life. We are declared holy by the blood of Jesus whenever we turn our hearts to God. That's justification and brings us into God's life. Now we're talking about the process of practical *sanctification*, where God makes us holy on the outside by transforming us.

What a marvelous process! God gives us a whole new perspective of life that frees us from pleasing ourselves and allows us to please him. Do you see how righteousness flows out of our relationship with God? We don't need to spend our efforts fighting sin—only on loving God.

Our part in that process is twofold. First, we must come often to enjoy God's presence so that we are filled with his perspectives. Second, we need to reckon ourselves dead to sin, no longer living for our own pleasure. Instead we can present ourselves to God as "instruments of righteousness." For this process to work that presentation must be practical. Every morning I offer the parts of my body to God in prayer. "Here are hands, feet, and voice for you to use today, Father, however you see fit."

Focusing on the Spirit's leading in our lives is a far more effective way to achieving righteousness than trying not to sin. If I asked you not to think about spinach for 15 seconds, you couldn't do it. In fact that's all you would think about. The same is true of sin. By trying to ignore temptation we fall victim to it. In Romans 7 Paul said that he did not even know what coveting was until he read the law that says "Do not covet." That command alone set him thinking about what he shouldn't be coveting, and he discovered a number of things he didn't have that he wanted. This attempt, Paul concluded, "produced in me every kind of covetous desire."

The same process also works with righteousness. As you behold God's glory and relate to him, you'll find yourself free from sin's clutches. In the time you were thinking "spinach" earlier, you probably didn't think once of strawberries. Haven't you known times when you were so enjoying God's touch in your life that days passed without you being aware of or fulfilling your sinful appetites? That's the renewal of the mind that only intimacy can produce.

That is the beauty of righteousness by faith. God will produce it in us as we love him. This is a process, and we shouldn't expect it to bring instant perfection. As we grow in intimacy we'll grow in righteousness. Whenever you find yourself in sin, confess it to God and determine to grow closer to him so that it will no longer win over you. But don't waste your time having feelings of condemnation that will only separate you from God and the healing he wants for you.

Five years ago severe chest pains drove me to the doctor. The diagnosis: stress induced by my profession. More accurately it should have been *stress induced by my response to my profession*. I was trying to obey God and still live up to our society's standards of a successful church. The paradox was killing me. I had trouble sleeping nights and was now plagued with chest pains.

The doctor told me to find another job, but when I asked God about it, he made it clear that it wasn't my job he wanted to change, but me. I sought God earnestly for healing, drawing closer to him than I ever had before. He started to work on that part of my flesh that seeks the approval of others.

So skillfully did God change that area of my life over the next year that I don't even remember when the pains and sleepless nights ceased. I only recognized that they had some months later when I was lying awake because of an athletic injury I had suffered earlier in the evening. Suddenly it dawned on me: I couldn't remember the last time I had lain awake, kept from sleep by my anxieties.

God had changed me, and the only thing I did differently was to draw closer to him. That is righteousness produced by faith. He gets the credit, not me. And now, whenever I find the old symptoms rising again, I need only look at my relationship with God and invariably I'll find that it has begun to slip, that I'm falling into religious patterns and losing the freshness of his presence.

Righteousness rising out of our relationship with God is the only way we will be changed. Everything else is just a placebo. It may trick us for a while, but the disease of sin still eats away at us from the inside. We may worry about people abusing this process, but no one really in love with Jesus and whose life is touched by him every day can help but be changed into his likeness.

The Fruit of Righteousness

Righteousness by faith is never something we'll be able to boast in, but it is something we can truly enjoy. It gives us a new perspective about everything around us. No longer will our quest for personal comfort hide God's work from us.

> Though outwardly we are wasting away, yet inwardly we are being renewed day by day. For our light and momentary troubles are achieving for us an eternal glory that far outweighs them all. So we fix our eyes not on what is seen, but on what is unseen. For what is seen is temporary, but what is unseen is eternal (2 Corinthians 4:16-18).

Here is the fruit of breaking the materialistic bonds that so distort our intimacy with God. The rise and fall of circumstances will no longer hold such power over our minds and emotions.

Living to please God will value eternal considerations over temporal ones. God's glory will be produced in us above our need for personal comfort, and the unseen spiritual world will be placed above the seen material one. With this perspective we will be able to see God more clearly and follow his objectives with greater certainty. All of this is produced by a simple hunger to be holy and a willingness to cooperate with God as he accomplishes his work in us.

As you follow him, you too will step back in surprise at the things he will change in you that right now look like insurmountable bondages. You will find the depth of true joy and happiness that result only from inheriting God's righteousness. It is truly one of God's greatest gifts.

Living
in the Joy of
Christian Community

15

Programmed to Death

THE LOSS OF THE PERSONAL TOUCH

They worship me in vain;
their teachings are but rules taught by men.
—Matthew 15:9

How easily Satan must have thought he could snuff out the light of God's kingdom in the world once Jesus had ascended to the Father! Only 120 followers remained, and they were huddled away in fear. Though the Day of Pentecost must have been a setback for him, he soon responded with a new strategy—bring in a heavy dose of persecution to extinguish the flame.

But it didn't work. Centuries of persecution followed, first by the religious leaders in Judea and later by the Roman emperors, but the church continued to thrive and expand. People discovered the power of the Risen Lord and at great cost surrendered their lives to him.

Sometime late in the third century Satan must have called a conclave. Hades I, he probably called it. Since persecution had failed so miserably, this diabolical council needed to develop a new strategy to undermine the life of the church. The solution it produced has done far more to render the church powerless than any persecution ever has.

The objectives were clear: The plan would have to diffuse the self-sacrificing love that carried the church through conflict, distract it from intimacy with God, and devalue the importance of the individual believer. And, since the church had already prevailed over direct assaults, the plan needed to be so deceptive that it could not be recognized as coming from hell.

A few suggestions were offered, but they were so weak that they didn't even invite discussion. After a painfully long silence, someone, perhaps Screwtape,[1] came up with a very simple idea: "Trying to keep it small hasn't worked—let's make it big!"

All the other devils gasped, thinking that old Screwtape had finally bolted his sanity. "Make it big? What do you think we've been working so hard to prevent?"

"Hear me out, colleagues. We can kill it with its own success. What would happen if the church suddenly became acceptable?"

"Lots of people would go to it, you idiot."

"But what would all those people do to it?" Screwtape replied with a smirk, then sat back as he watched their minds churn. One-by-one the others began to see the brilliance of his scheme.

"Many would come just for social reasons. They would quickly dilute those who are really in God's clutches."

"And imagine all the programs and activities they would have to plan to keep those people happy. Nothing chokes out intimacy as well as busyness."

"A crowd like that would have opinions so diverse and disruptive that the power of the gospel would be compromised in just a few short years."

"The church would eventually become a machine, chewing up individuals instead of loving them. Programs would take over where personal ministries now flourish. And everyone knows how easy it is to kill a program."

"Hear! Hear!" they all yelled.

"They couldn't possibly teach all the followers to walk with God personally, so they would soon substitute rules and guidelines for his ever-present voice."

"The machine would have to be run by professionals. The others would become nothing more than spectators and bill-payers."

"And that leadership would waste most of its time tied up in administration, which we know benefits almost no one."

"Who would have time for individuals? They would have to try to disciple people by regulations, and the cracks in that are so wide we could go on vacation."

"And best of all," Screwtape spoke up again, "they wouldn't even know what had happened to them. They would think themselves successful beyond their wildest dreams. They would be pillars in the community and stand before huge crowds. We would let them keep all their Christian terms, but we would substitute our own meanings. It's foolproof!"

"But size alone won't do that, Screwtape," Satan himself finally said. "They could still teach all those people what it really means to follow God and they could still love people one-by-one no matter how big it got."

"True, O Wicked One," Screwtape waggled his index finger, "but do you think they would? Do you think they would risk losing all those people or would resist the corruption that such power and influence would give them?"

Satan smiled in whatever ecstasy hell allows. "Of course not!" He slammed his fist on the table, "Let's do it!"

The Ravages of Institutionalism

Throughout the third and fourth centuries persecution against Christianity declined. Through the reign of Constantine the church was granted freedom of worship. Further privileges followed, until in 380 Theodosius I made Christianity the state religion of the Roman Empire. But what looked like a great victory for Christianity proved to be its greatest challenge. Though its new position brought truth and morality to Roman culture, the arrogance of political power subverted the church's spirituality. It even degenerated into spreading the truth by force, first over the barbarians and in later centuries through the Crusades and the Inquisition. The persecuted became the persecutor.

Even a cursory look at church history demonstrates that wherever the church has undergone persecution and martyrdom its vitality has risen sharply, and wherever it finds social acceptability and comfort, though its statistics increase, its potency diminishes rapidly. It becomes ensnared in institutional concerns to the distraction of intimacy with God.

Much has been written in the last few decades about the church being an organism and not an organization. We are comfortable with that theology, but the models are hard to find. Just saying it doesn't make it so. Our institutions are so demanding that professionals carry the bulk of ministry and believers are reduced to mere spectators.

In Frank Herbert's *Dune Messiah* an entire religion is created to sustain the rule of an Emperor over a vast segment of the universe. The Qizarate were the civil servants responsible to oversee the spread of the "religious" element of the empire. Herbert uses this institution to poke fun at religion in general and Christianity in particular, an attack not wholly undeserved. Describing one of their number, Herbert said:

> His goals were Routine and Records. . . . Expedience was the first word in his catechism . . . but he betrayed by every action that he preferred machines to men, statistics to individuals, the far away general view to the intimate personal touch requiring imagination and initiative.[2]

How quickly and easily it happens, again and again, not just to the historical church but to individual believers! We start out with the excitement of following Jesus and loving his people but end up shuffling records and making rules. Howard Snyder probably summed up this urge best: "Like the children of Israel in the desert we yearn for the predictable, safe bondage of institutional captivity."[3]

Why? Probably the biggest reason is that institutionalism is a part of our society. Humans love playing with organizations, and when believers stop changing the world they tend to become like it. Charles Hummel called it the Chameleon Effect:

> In every age the church tends to take on the colors of its culture. . . . Modern man has become obsessed with technique, with procedures and methods to get results in the most efficient way. . . . In concentrating on the means, we have lost sight of the ends,

> even in dealing with others. We should use things and love people; but we love things and use people. They have become one more means—a stepping-stone or ladder—to our own end.[4]

Even if our ends are noble, institutionalism will never accomplish the work of God. This is not to say that it won't have some positive effects, but that it will always fall short and leave people bruised and hurt. Jesus and the early church both kept structures to a minimum, preferring the power of the Spirit and the relationships between believers to provide ministry.

Another reason we fall so easily into the pit of institutionalism is that it allows us to stay in control. It is easier to plan seminars, vacation Bible schools, and new building projects than it is to get involved in personal ministry situations that demand the effective presence of Jesus. For the same reason Israel constantly turned to Egypt when threatened, finding their aid more tangible than God's.

> Woe to those who go down to Egypt for help, who rely on horses, who trust in the multitude of their chariots and in the great strength of their horsemen, but do not look to the Holy One of Israel, or seek help from the Lord (Isaiah 31:1).

How tragic that the resources of this world are easier to trust in than the activity of our God! His activity is perceived by many people to be too capricious. They would rather ask him to bless their efforts than rely on his. God is not capricious; yet, as with Israel, our inattentiveness to him makes it seem so. We have ended up like them, confident only in the things we control.

Institutionalism appeals to our need to be busy, and there's nothing more intoxicating to some people than the adrenaline released by running a smooth operation. I've been in a position where eight decisions demanded my immediate attention, with two phone calls holding and a counseling appointment in the lobby. It's exhilarating, and the appreciation expressed by many people for our efforts is part of the brew—but the rush of personal importance has nothing to do with the affirmation of the Spirit.

Terrific programs rarely lead to changed lives, and we've committed altogether too much power to them. Howard Snyder comments:

> Such institutionalized churches attempt vainly to minister through ever improved and expanding programs, training and techniques. Under unusually talented leadership such churches succeed, and everyone praises that success and uses it as a model. But in the majority of cases such spiritual technology fails, and only leaves local members frustrated, starving for real spiritual fellowship.[5]

Institutional efforts can provide the guise of success even where the life of Jesus isn't real. That's what is so deceptive about it. We think we're pleasing God for all our activity and its results, yet beneath the programs and entertainment lies an emptiness that few will admit. Leaders burn out, stress out, or get lost in sin. How often have we seen supposedly successful leaders fall to deception, greed, or immorality! How many more will we yet see? Institutionalism allows us to feel good about ourselves even after our responsiveness to God has ceased.

This problem with institutionalism could be easily resolved if we could declare structures evil and abandon them entirely. But, like the person on a diet, the true challenge is not total abstinence but moderation. *Some* structure is essential for believers to cooperate together—exactly how much is the question. Gluttony is a preoccupation with food over nourishment; institutionalism is a preoccupation with structure over substance. Both confuse the end with the means and in doing so lead to the opposite results of what they intend.

Finding the right mix demands vigilance. When we've swallowed too much institutionalism in God's name we need to recognize that our efforts have become counterproductive.

The Symptoms of Institutionalism

Institutionalism is not hard to detect. Whatever it touches is infected with at least one of the following six symptoms. We'll look at each one to see how it has infiltrated twentieth-century Christianity. Even more important, we need to see how these symptoms are infecting our personal life and intimacy with God.

Pragmatism. Watch carefully whenever people tell you, "This is what we have to do to get the job done." Usually what they are defending is offensive to any rational person, but because they want the result so badly they are willing to be pragmatic about the means, using whatever works.

After being criticized, one Christian television talk-show host defended the program's use of gimmickry and emotionalism in fund-raising appeals by saying, "Tell me what else we can do. We have to do it this way because we have no other option." A regent of a major Christian university replied to me about promising donors specific blessings from God in return for their offerings: "Wayne, it works and it must be done, so we can't be afraid to use it."

The same pragmatism is used when pastors refuse to speak the truth boldly for fear that people might be offended. Their logic goes something like this: If I say it, people might leave. If they leave, we won't be able to make our building payment. That would be a bad witness to the community; therefore God wouldn't want me to deal with it now.

Pragmatism substitutes natural wisdom for God's wisdom and puts our own survival above his righteousness. The eye focused on the bottom line will not find God's leading. Anything needing to be kept alive by sacrifices on the altar of pragmatism deserves to die. But that is a difficult choice, and history teaches us that pragmatism can easily keep an organization going long after God has ceased to participate in it.

Buildings and budget. After witnessing the glory of Jesus transfigured before Moses and Elijah on the mountain, Peter uses the opportunity to stick his foot in his mouth: "Master, it is good for us to be here. Let us put up three shelters—one for you, one for Moses and one for Elijah." Both Mark and Luke include a parenthetical explanation after Peter's outburst: "He did not know what he was saying. They were so frightened."

I don't know what it is about believers that drives them to build buildings, but Luke flatly said that it comes from ignorance and fear. I can believe that. When an evangelist or church can think of nothing else to do, they draw up plans for a new building and beg people for the money to build it. Fund-raisers admit that it is easier to raise money for a new building than anything else. Architect's renderings and scale models seem to stimulate generosity. They won't admit it publicly, but some evangelists have even built buildings they didn't need merely to boost income.

The Word indicates nothing against believers having places to meet in, and I'm not against them either. But today Christianity seems plagued with a fetish for luxurious buildings. When we think our construction projects are synonymous with ministry, we've slipped over the line. So complete is this distortion that one TV evangelist tried to convince his followers that God was waiting to pour out a worldwide revival until his new international headquarters building was completed.

Can you imagine people believing that? They did—even though nothing happened once it was completed. Neither Jesus nor the early church ever had a building to call their own, but their ministries never suffered because of it.

Outsiders and insiders alike feel the strain of the church's preoccupation with money and buildings. Fund-raising has become a science, and those who do it today know that it works best if a mailing includes three pieces of mail, blue underlining in the main letter, a punchy P.S. at the end, and an offer of a cheap trinket or a blessing from God for those who respond. "Experts in greed," Peter said of false teachers, and our efforts to motivate people to give by guilt or prestige are no different.

Money and buildings, though useful, are not essential. A ministry that demands them in order to be successful misunderstands the heart of ministry itself.

Mass production. Why is it that we demand teacher/student ratios at our schools of 25:1 but crave 2000:1 in our churches? Can we really expect to put 2000 people in a room, give them a lecture from the Bible, and expect them to learn intimacy? Jesus obviously thought that 12:1 was more realistic, and he shaped the lives of those who followed him as much by his example as by his teachings.

Because our leadership-to-learner ratio is so large, we try to stamp disciples out like mass-produced computer chips. Instead of providing models for growing believers and the opportunity to get specific questions answered, we fill them with outlines and principles.

The most obvious symptom of a mass-production mentality is an obsession with statistics. No question yields less significant information about a church than "How big is it?" Yet no question is more often asked than this. In our day it has led to a new field of academic study called "church growth." It counts people in pews, baptisms, and parking spaces—anything that gives credibility to our efforts as the measure of success. Though such counting may be well-intentioned, I've seen nothing affect pastors more adversely. It pressures pastors to meet false standards of success, and it encourages pragmatism and efficiency over building disciples. You don't need to count numbers in order to have a heart to see new people come to the Lord.

No matter how inspirational they might be, lectures alone won't make disciples. Christians cannot be mass-produced any more than human babies can. They need a living example nearby to show them how to follow Christ, to answer their questions, and to pray them through needs. For that to happen, however, more people must be equipped to nurture new believers and to spend the time essential to help them grow.

Efficiency. As institutionalism takes over, one survival mode soon becomes the basis for all decision-making: efficiency. How can we accomplish as much as possible with as little time and expense as possible? "Dead weight" is jettisoned so that the machine is not impaired by any one person's particular need or weakness. But what is efficient for the majority is ineffective for the individual. United Airlines may be able to take me around the world, but it can't get me from Visalia to San Francisco. That demands a less-efficient commuter line, more tailored to my needs.

Jesus never demonstrated an all-out passion for efficiency. He could have held a crusade in downtown Samaria to minister to hundreds of people instead of wasting his time at the well with only one woman. But if he had held a crusade, this woman wouldn't have been there. She was too immoral and too wrapped up in religious controversies. She needed a personal invitation into God's life. Love is not "efficient," and when churches become efficient they end up loveless.

A search for efficiency leads to a challengeless gospel and a false discipleship. Church-growth experts tell us that homogeneous groups are more efficient: "All men like to become Christians in their own social groupings, without crossing barriers. Every man should be able to become a Christian with his own kind of people."[6]

Peter Wagner explains that "churches grow when they concentrate on only one homogeneous unit. Show me a growing church and I will show you a homogeneous-unit church."[7] Whatever happened to the slave and free, rich and poor worshiping together? If people do not want to be converted in that setting, maybe we need to assess the quality of their conversion. How does this approach differ from Peter leaving the Gentiles' table to sit with the Jews? It was wrong for him and wrong for us not to challenge people with diverse relationships in the body of Christ.

Generalization. Institutions by nature deal with people as groups and not individuals. Crowds reduce people to the lowest common denominator and set the climate for helping people by guidelines and rules. Some people in fact may be helped, but many more fall through the cracks. Conclusions for the masses rarely hammer out so easily in individual lives. To generalize with people's lives is to offer them less ministry than Jesus did.

Marketing. As much as Paul speaks of God's grace that absolutely negates personal boasting, institutions thrive on it. Public relations (and continued financial support) demand that we claim God is working a special way through our ministries. Look through any Christian magazine or the church page of a local paper and you'll find ad after ad boasting about the way our church, school, association, or pastor's seminar is accomplishing great things for God. Fundraising letters are filled with such boasting, while at the same time they cover up their failures, mistakes, and hurts in the name of furthering the gospel. Why is no one appalled by such a system?

Our problems are further compounded by marketing Christianity itself. It has become such a profitable business that people become part of Christianity for reasons other than service to Jesus. Our lecture circuits and talk shows hold lucrative offers for both pocket and ego. Today "gospel" outsells most other kinds of music. We have our own toys, laundry soap, and yellow pages. Before we congratulate ourselves for being so opportunistic, perhaps we should heed Os Guiness' call to look deeper.

> We evangelicals today make the money changers look like bungling amateurs the way we have turned faith into products to be sold in the marketplace. Their use of television, marketing styles and so on is incredibly uncritical and profoundly worldly.[8]

Out of the Institutional Trap

"My people have committed two sins: They have forsaken me, the spring of living water, and have dug their own cisterns." That is the result of succumbing to the pressures of institutionalism. We lose God's presence and substitute for it with water dug out of our own efforts. Though this pacifies many people, it never achieves what it promises and instead leaves people hurt and disillusioned.

In the third book of Frank Herbert's *Dune* series a prophet returns to the religious hierarchy with a warning that the church today also needs to hear:

> I mean to disturb you! It is my intention! I come here to combat the fraud and illusion of your conventional, institutionalized religion. As with all such religions your institution moves toward cowardice, it moves toward mediocrity, inertia and self-satisfaction.[9]

This chapter is not intended to be a sweeping condemnation of all institutional structures or of all people involved in them. Some people are finding a vital relationship with God in the midst of them, and for that I am grateful. But not everyone has been so fortunate. Many people are being torn apart by our institutional objectives, and altogether too much ministry to the individual has been lost because we have been too busy baby-sitting the machine. The Christianity that institutionalism produces bears little of Christ's image.

Jesus called us to life in him that demands authenticity, that frees ministry from financial constraints, and that releases people to ministry instead of capturing them with it. He taught us to love in the singular—"one another"—and not through intricately planned programs. He warned us not to bask in personal notoriety but to ascribe all glory to him. For too long the church has been held captive by its seduction with size and success.

Truly effective ministry will pull away from big ministries, opulent buildings, and successful systems. Our only objective should be to build "living temples" (Ephesians 2:19-22) so that we "present everyone perfect in Christ" (Colossians 1:28). This agenda demands the presence of Jesus and the freedom of the Holy Spirit to move beyond our institutional concerns.

God wants people to be touched personally. He penetrates hearts, not programs. That's what intimacy is all about, and it is what we are called to pass on to others. That's the Christianity that threatens hell's gates and answers people's deepest cries.

16

The New Testament Community

RESTORING THE PERSONAL TOUCH

In him you too are being built together
to become a dwelling
in which God lives by his Spirit.
—Ephesians 2:22

Recapturing the personal aspect of Jesus' ministry will not be easy in an age that regards a computer-addressed form letter to be a personal touch. "I care about each of you personally and want to hear from you," the evangelist says into a camera lens, and we've come to believe him even though he knows nothing about us. And how personal can church life be when we're herded in and out of services like amusement park junkies?

We're so used to mass-produced ministry that we actually think it can carry the same love and compassion to 10,000 people at once that Jesus took individually to the Samaritan woman at the well, Simon Peter in his boat, or Nicodemus with his questions. It cannot. Large-group ministry can be valuable to encourage, instruct, and challenge people, but it alone will not transform people.

One of the greatest problems that believers face today is unfulfilled expectations. They know what God wants for them, but not how to get there. How many people do you know who live in the frustration of unconquered sin, a suffering loved one, or the inability to walk in the peace or joy they know Christ offers? How many more do you think mask their feelings well enough so you'll never know? They either blame themselves and are swallowed up in guilt or else blame God, thinking him unjust. No one has ever taken the time to make the life of Jesus real for them.

Jesus demonstrated the fact that practical change comes out of personal contact. Though he preached to crowds he got down to business in one-on-one and small-group encounters. Here people could be treated as individuals and lives could be shaped in the reality of their own questions and needs.

"There's no way the church can take the time to touch people that personally" is the oft-heard excuse. And it's a true one, too, if we're talking of structures, programs, and leadership doing all the personal ministry. The Word, however, challenges us to a church life where everyone is involved, giving and receiving from one another as friends and partners in the gospel. Only through this kind of community can the church recapture the personal touch essential to discipleship and evangelism.

That's what inspired David Watson, who has called the church back to her first-century example as passionately as anyone:

> [Jesus] called the Twelve to share their lives, with him and with each other. They were to live every day in a rich and diverse fellowship, losing independence, learning interdependence, gaining from each other new riches and strength. They were to share everything—joys, sorrows, pains and possessions—to become the community of Christ the King.[1]

The Challenge of Community

The parable of the lost sheep has not always been one of my favorites. The shepherd leaves 99 seemingly perfect sheep to look for the foolish one who wandered away from the flock. I grew up in church and always remember wanting to serve God. I never wandered into blatant sin, yet I saw newly saved addicts, murderers, and immoral celebrities rewarded with book contracts and TV interviews. I was one of the neglected 99 because I had never been dumb enough to turn my back on God.

Only later did I learn that Jesus wasn't saying he would neglect his followers to find sinners, but was demonstrating how singularly God can be involved in each one of our lives. The 99 were not followers of Jesus at all, but were the self-righteous who thought themselves too good for a Savior. They didn't lack the need—only the awareness of it.

Augustine said that God loved us so much he would have sent his Son if there had been only one person to save. That is the point of this parable, not just for salvation but for everything else about our lives. God doesn't primarily love crowds or groups of people; an infinite God can love in the singular—one at a time. He says he loves all the world because he loves each person in it. He doesn't love you because he's committed to love all humans as a group; he loves you as an individual person, created for his glory.

If we're going to mirror this love in the body of Christ we will have to avoid investing it in institutions. People's needs are just too important and too unique to commit to the rigidity of a program. The efforts of institutions are limited at best, for they exist for crowds, not individuals, and appeal to people at the lowest common denominator.

Community, on the other hand, is God loving people through each other as they respond to the uniqueness of the moment and the moving of the Holy Spirit. Biblical community does not suppress the individual for the good of the whole; it is keenly aware of how uniquely God works with people and desires to enhance that work in others.

Community can begin only in God's presence. Personal care is the overflow of that relationship. That's why the gatherings of the church must be structured so that people can share together God's real presence. As we worship him from our hearts, he will come to show himself by Word and Spirit. Nothing could be more exciting than this, and the love spawned in that setting will have the flexibility to convey God's love to people whether they are a growing disciple or an unbeliever trapped in the world's darkness.

Community cannot be brought about by coercion. It must be freely chosen and lived out daily, like everything else about our faith. Many people in recent years, not understanding the need for voluntary participation, have tried to enforce community among believers. Some methods are so stringent that they have shattered the lives of the people who were supposed to be helped. The biblical goal was supplanted by unbiblical methodology. Community can result only from the Spirit of God stirring people to submit their lives to one another. Nothing can short-circuit this, even though it means that the quality of community may often be sporadic.

One of the reasons we cling to "ministry by program" even though it is ineffective is because it is at least easy. Only a few people need to be motivated to do it, and most of them can be paid for their efforts. They make our rules and coordinate an enjoyable program. If someone's spiritual life does not get better it can be blamed on his lack of participation. That is much easier than making the gospel effective in individual lives.

Programmed ministry offers a minimum dose of personal confrontation or responsibility. Small groups work poorly in America because people "won't like to work in such a way. It takes time and money and energy and they will have to sacrifice their private time."[2]

We have confused independence with freedom. To live by our own desires, to ignore the input of others, to care only about our own needs—these are the tools of darkness.

Jesus said that freedom is found only in truth and that truth is found only as it rises out of believers loving God together and sharing their wisdom and insight with each other. Unfortunately, few people have had church experiences that match this biblical objective. Many have been brutalized by the political infighting, malicious gossip, and conflicting egos that dominate much of church life today.

The church is notorious for shooting its wounded and putting its rookies on the front line (saving the fluff jobs for those who by seniority have "earned" it). We do more damage to ourselves than we have ever done to the gates of hell. Honest confession of sin is lost because such confession is usually used to judge rather than to forgive and cleanse. Expressed needs are regarded as evidence of immaturity instead of as opportunities to share the load.

Our own disgust at the loss of personal love in the church is evidence that we have a better hope. It is time for us to find out how to make that hope come true. We have no choice; the world is no longer impressed by our buildings and programs. They are looking for exactly what Jesus said they would—genuine love expressed between believers.

The Context for Community

No one told the early church to form a community. I can't imagine the disciples gathering on Pentecost evening trying to figure out what to do with 3120 people. Can you see Peter suggesting an idea like this?

> Let's have everyone meet together on Sunday mornings and we'll organize home groups for midweek. Andrew and Nathaniel, find us the natural leaders out of this group and take them on a retreat this weekend. They'll lead groups for us. Thomas, draw up some guidelines for participation and we'll have people sign them. We'll require attendance and the rich to sell their property to help the poor. . . .

Absurd, isn't it? Without anyone even thinking of organizing, the church became a caring community that was worshiping and growing together. The people shared resources so well that there were no needy among them. Even secular historians of the time marveled at the love they had for each other.

Though the models of such community may be few today, what institutional priorities have destroyed can be regained by hungry people:

> If the church is to become a community of God's people . . . it means much more than singing the

same hymns, praying the same prayers, taking the
same sacraments and joining in the same services. It
will involve the full commitment of our lives, and of
all that we have, to one another. It is only as we lose
our lives that we find them, so bringing the life of
Jesus to others.[3]

Why is it so hard for the church today to recapture what
came so naturally to the early church? Simply because they
knew they needed it and we don't think we do. Community
rises out of the convergence of two different streams. Identi-
fying them in the early church can help us rediscover them
today.

1. *Their love for God.* The church started with 3000 people,
all of whom were overwhelmed by a fresh experience of the
reality and love of God. I've often thought how the body life of
the fellowship I pastor would differ if we could all capture that
first love on the same day. The joy would be infectious, and so
would the hunger to learn the ways of God.

That joy and hunger are the foundation of community.
Without it everything else is merely an exercise in human
relations and will not ultimately rise to the splendor of biblical
community. Jesus prayed that all his followers would find
unity together, but even his prayer makes it clear that there is
only one road to unity: "I have given them the glory that you
gave me, that they may be one as we are one" (John 17:22).

The unity that marks Christian community cannot rise out
of charity, compromise, or concession. It rises only out of
people who are seeking to be changed into God's image. As
God is changing me, I find tremendous compatibility with
others he is also changing. Without even trying, I'm suddenly
aware of their needs and how I can help, and I'm also conscious of the insight they can add to my life.

Community is the result of intimacy and the environment
in which it grows. Scripture links our spiritual health to
community involvement with other believers. Only believers
who can speak the truth in love with each other "will in all

things grow up into him who is the Head" (Ephesians 4:15); and only by being "encouraged in heart and united in love" can we "have the full riches of complete understanding" (Colossians 2:2).

For people hungering after God, opening their lives to others is not a cumbersome obedience but a valuable resource of encouragement, strength, and confirmation.

2. *The reality of their struggle.* Imagine yourself awakening on a forest floor, your head racked with pain. For a moment you can't remember where you are or why you hurt so badly. Looking around in the increasing light of early dawn, you note the wispy columns of smoke rising from the twisted wreckage. You see the clearing carved out by the plane's descent and crash. Then you remember the exploding antiaircraft shells in the pitch-black sky around you, a violent jolt, a sharp left descending turn. The plane's pitch was too steep to bail out until that final flare-out over the trees.

Moans of pain call you back to the present. There are other survivors—ten, to be exact, from your mission team—but you're far from your objective, with injuries and without supplies. Since you are 200 miles inside enemy lines, the only rescue party you can expect will make you prisoners of war.

Now *there's* a context for body life! Such men aren't going to fight for position or waste time complaining about their circumstances. All their energies will be channeled into continuing with their mission if possible, and if not, then into creating havoc for the enemy while they try to get back across enemy lines. They'll mold each man's gifts and abilities into a team that stands the best possible chance of achieving their goal.

The early church understood the desperate reality of their circumstances, and their cooperation with each other matched that perception. Jesus had warned them how fragile his life was in a world that is hostile toward God and filled with an enemy bent on their destruction. They shared and ministered without the petty political concerns that normally drain church life. They were in occupied country, endeavoring to please God when they knew that so much in them wanted to please themselves.

No one told them they needed each other; they just knew it. Circumstances haven't changed—only our perception of them. We are still at war. Casualties line our streets and the enemy encircles us with his forces, but we don't see it. The reason that church life today is caught in so many organizational headaches and is dragged down by the ambitions of others is because it realizes neither the desperateness of its situation nor the fragility of its life.

Community is a *practical* response, not a philosophical one. When you need God desperately you'll find yourself teaming up with others who do too—for the mutual benefit of all.

The Joy of Community

We've already highlighted a number of the benefits of community, including personal care, increased wisdom, and shared resources. But there is one other benefit that stands above the rest—the joy and freshness of the spontaneous work of God among his people. No organizational plan can ever achieve the sheer beauty of people doing what needs to be done by the direction of the Holy Spirit instead of simply filling an institutional role.

The ministry of that first flock was carried by such spontaneity of the Spirit. People's needs were met, revivals of salvation broke out, and missionaries were sent out—all by his leading. The church thrived without the benefit of computers, bulletins, organization manuals, and committee meetings. Today our structures demand that our leaders spend more than 75 percent of their time entangled in administrative tasks.

I remember when my parents and their friends first discovered God's reality. People flocked to our home every Friday night to sing, pray, and share what the Lord was doing in them, often going late into the night. Excitement abounded. Eventually those people were forced out of their church and started their own. No more Friday night meetings; now it was services Sunday morning, Sunday evening, and midweek. Boards were elected and programs planned—and the excitement quickly vanished.

Community lets us share the joy of God's spontaneity. In the last few years this goal has led the fellowship in which I pastor to make a host of changes in the way we operate. We recognized that the services and activities we planned and executed with the greatest precision never rose to the level of fruitfulness we had anticipated. What's more, other activities that we had planned with less concern for form, or that we were caught in without warning, were profoundly alive with God's presence and power. With such experiences it's no wonder that we've come to trust people simply obeying God to lead to greater fruitfulness than our most finely produced program.

I've noticed this same thing to be true in other organizations and their ministries. I never really understood why until I read the observations of another pilgrim, Arthur Blessitt. His unique call has taken him around the world, carrying a 12-foot wooden cross as a testimony to Jesus Christ. In his autobiography he sums up one of his observations about his journeys under the cross:

> It seems that in many places response is easy, deep, and powerful as well as life-changing. But where there is high expectation, finer organization, promotion and long-planned prayer meetings, what is worked so hard for, I seldom see the event live up to the expectation. The glory of God seems to be revealed most powerfully and the response seems to be the greatest when things happen spontaneously and flow from simplicity, when everything that happens [is] attributed to God and to Him alone. It is like God will not share his glory with anyone.[4]

I realize that some people may misunderstand this thought as an excuse to be lazy and careless in God's work, but they shouldn't. Flowing with God's Spirit in the spontaneity of the moment requires greater diligence than any institutional program ever requires. The excellence we press for is not in the tasks of planning, administrating, and communicating, but in intimacy, obedience, and love.

There is a price to be paid for the spontaneity that community engenders, but it's well worth it. There's nothing more enjoyable than being with people so in love with God that they don't need programs to entertain or motivate them. Out of the fullness of their own love for God they care for each other and reach out to the lost with great simplicity and effectiveness.

The Cost of Community

I've worked around one simple point in this entire chapter: Community can only happen among disciples—people desiring to be changed by Christ into his image. The reason that community is so elusive is because most church meetings are geared to people who only nominally want to serve God.

There's nothing wrong with the church having meetings where this kind of people can be touched, but to pass it off as the life of the church is grossly inaccurate. Such people are too carnal to discover the depth of relationships which Jesus wants to build between believers. In catering to them with our structures we destroy community. Robert Girard, who paid a severe price in trying to change his congregation from an institution to a community (documented in his two books, *Brethren, Hang Loose* and *Brethren, Hang Together*), comments:

> The institutionalization of the church almost invariably strives to make the inefficient and costly process of building and maintaining open, loving personal relationships with one another "unnecessary." We seem committed to setting the church's organizational machinery up in such a way that it will roll on quite nicely without either trust or love.[5]

No wonder our efforts end in confusion, anger, and lack of participation! You can't build community out of anything but disciples; but having them, no one needs to build it at all.

Believers who have been to the cross together will walk away from it ready to discover the joy of community:

> The cross is the heart of all fellowship, and it is only through the cross that fellowship is deepened and matured. This will involve the frequent and painful crucifixion of self in all its forms—self-seeking, self-centeredness, self-righteousness—and the willingness to remain vulnerable in open fellowship with other Christians.[6]

Challenging the tyranny of self is at the same time the cost of community and one of its greatest gifts. Since self diminishes our ability to perceive God, denying it leads to deeper relationships with God as well as with other people.

If we can affirm the following statements which the Bible makes about our relationships with others, we'll find ourselves quite naturally moving toward the depths of community.

1. I don't have all the answers. I can only understand clearly what Jesus is doing in my life when it stands alongside the work he is doing in other members of the body (1 Corinthians 12).

2. The church can only be effective when each member is contributing his part. Ministry by a few will never be complete (Ephesians 4:16).

3. I will only grow in maturity when other believers are in a place to speak lovingly and honestly with me (Ephesians 4:15).

4. I cannot make it alone. The real challenges of this age supersede my own exclusive relationship with God. Often my battles need the aid and support of other soldiers in God's army (Matthew 18:19,20).

5. Other people's needs are as important as my own (Philippians 2:4), and all my gifts and resources are at God's disposal, to use as he sees fit (Acts 4:32).

When you understand these statements you'll seek for relationships that fulfill them. Get together with other disciples in settings where you can effectively touch each other's lives. Often this will be in small enough groups that each individual has a sense of his significance and responsibility to the others. Such a group can be as small as three or as large as 50 or 60, depending on the relationships involved.

Take care to ensure that these relationships don't grow exclusive or stale. Through hospitality and outreach continue to meet new people and extend to them the fellowship of the Spirit, looking for ways you can be a blessing to them.

Though the depths of biblical community are still largely uncharted waters for the Western believer, they should still be sailed. The testimony by others of its vitality and life is well-documented. It's time to shake ourselves from the selfishness that so easily and subtly distracts us from one another.

Best of all, you need not wait for your church to start a new program. You can begin with some believers you know who are ready to grow in the Lord together. As God puts your lives together you'll find joy so deep that you'll wonder how you ever thought all the programs could replace or even stimulate such love!

Drawing from God's Power

17

Where Has All the Power Gone?

THE LOSS OF SUPERNATURAL POWER

Awake, awake, O Zion;
clothe yourself with strength.
Put on your garments of splendor.
—Isaiah 52:1

Whether or not people liked Jesus or agreed with him, the thing that most impressed them was his sense of authority. Even his enemies marveled at the power that flowed from his life. And that is an amazing statement about a man who had no wealth, political clout, or wide following. Jesus drew his authority from a far deeper well.

People saw it in the synagogues where he taught simple lessons: "They were amazed at his teaching, because he taught them as one who had authority" (Matthew 7:28,29).

They saw it when he cast out evil spirits with just a word. The people wondered, "What is this? A new teaching—and with authority! He even gives orders to evil spirits and they obey him" (Mark 1:27).

They saw it when he rebuked the violent storm on the Sea of Galilee and immediately it grew calm. "What kind of man is this? Even the wind and the waves obey him!" (Matthew 8:27).

Jesus had authority where it counted. It didn't reside in his mannerisms, volume, or charisma, but in this simple fact: What he said and what he did made a difference.

Scripture makes no suggestion that Jesus was a flamboyant orator. Yet his hearers knew they were being talked to at a level that no one else had ever approached—not the scribes in all their wisdom, not the Pharisees in their arrogance, not even Pilate in his regal court. Jesus' recorded sermons were only simple stories and direct challenges.

Yet his authority was evident in two aspects. First, he spoke the truth clearly and directly, with the conviction of heart that

demonstrated to people that he fully believed and lived up to
what he said. Though he spoke in love, he didn't obscure the
truth for fear of offending people. Everyone knew what he
said and what it would cost them to believe him.

Second, he also made truth live. He said that God cared
about people whom the enemy had crushed, and he showed it
by healing a leper. He forgave sins, and lame people walked
away healed.

There is no greater symptom of the church's nakedness
than its loss of this simple authority. While our theology may
be sound, it is distorted by the fact that it doesn't seem to make
a difference in the lives of those who believe it. We talk about
how much God loves people, and we trust that this knowledge
alone is their help—instead of showing them how effective
God's love can be in changing their lives.

The victims that such a gospel leaves are many. When theology cannot be measured in human experience, people will
quickly grow disillusioned and cold. How can we expect people
to believe in God's love if they never see any practical expression of it? Would we trust a friend who says he loves us if he
never helps us when we are in trouble? Of course not. Love
expresses itself in *action*, and we naturally expect no less of
God until someone trains us otherwise.

Jesus gave his generation a gospel teeming with supernatural power. He committed that same thing to his disciples:
He told them to go out preaching the gospel while healing the
sick, freeing captives, and raising the dead. Would he ask us to
offer anything less?

If he hasn't, where has all the power gone?

A Loving God in a Painful World

Time after time, I have seen families and even
whole communities unite in prayer for the recovery
of a sick person, only to have their hopes and prayers
mocked. I have seen the wrong people get sick, the
wrong people be hurt, the wrong people die young.[1]

Though few would express it as harshly, I think most people have felt similarly at times. Rabbi Harold Kushner's *When Bad Things Happen to Good People* was another attempt to answer a question that has nagged mankind since the beginning: How can a loving God be in charge of such a painful world?

Those who do not believe in God often cite this excuse as a swaying argument. Why did God allow the tortures of the Inquisition, slavery in the U.S., or Hitler's holocaust? Does his inactivity condone apartheid in South Africa, persecution in the Eastern Bloc, or starvation in Africa? Closer to home, why doesn't he prevent the tragedies and sicknesses that take our loved ones prematurely?

Nothing forces people to contemplate theology as much as suffering does. Is there a God? If so, what kind of God is he? One mother expressed this question in the frustration of dealing with her son's violent behavior at school and home. He had been normal until his father had tragically died. "Why couldn't I control Buddy? Anger ate at me. I was mad at Buddy. And myself. And the principal. And Paul, for dying. And God, for permitting it."[2]

That's where people usually think they find God—always in the background, either orchestrating, allowing, or at least ignoring. Even those who deny his existence will cry out in pain or crisis in hopes that they might be wrong. The odds may seem like a celestial lottery, but what have you got to lose when every other possibility has been exhausted?

Other people, a bit more confident in their relationship with God, approach God with greater expectancy, though often with no better results. If God is real, why doesn't he take a more active hand in our crises? Three conclusions have been suggested.

1. *God doesn't exist.* The atheist sees life as only the random action of matter. Some get the breaks, others only hard luck. You can't expect God to bail you out, so do the best you can. Though such thinking makes life easier to understand, it doesn't work. God is real. Not only did Jesus show us the reality of God when he was here, but most people when truly

honest will admit to some moment in their past when they touched a presence greater than themselves. They may not have honored him as God, but they know he's there.

2. *God is not all-loving.* He may exist, but he ignores our pain. Some people suggest that he is concerned with far greater things and that it is prideful for us to ask for his help. Others suggest that God is somehow restricted from supernatural intervention in this dispensation. But the most painful form of this idea is when it attacks the sufferer personally. God might help others, but he doesn't care about me.

No matter what disguise this philosophy appears in, it challenges the heart of God's nature and leads to guilt and isolation. If God's love cannot be expressed to us practically, what good is it?

3. *God is not all-powerful.* This is the answer that Kushner advances. Sin has brought so much chaos into the world that not even God can make order out of it. Kushner's approach is a compassionate and pragmatic one; it tries to save us from the anguish of the false expectation that bad things happen only to bad people, and from guilt when our prayers for relief go unanswered. He concludes that God loves us deeply and will help us handle crises but is powerless to change tragic circumstances.

Kushner's attempt at compassionate pragmatism fails, however, because God is all-powerful. I too sympathize with those whose confidence in God's justice is devoured by their pain and whose security in his love is thwarted by unanswered prayer. But giving them a loving though powerless God certainly can't help.

The Word paints a different picture entirely, and presents the reason why people expect more than this from God. The Old Testament is full of stories of God intervening to help people, and Jesus demonstrated a God who cared about each individual—his sin, his pain, his sicknesses. He even said that his miracles were proof that God's kingdom had broken into human history for the express purpose of redeeming the anguish that sin has produced in our world.

But would this power continue after Jesus ascended to God? The scriptural evidence is overpowering. Throughout Acts and the Epistles miraculous signs and physical healings filled the life of the church.

Peter, Stephen, Philip, and Paul performed great miracles and healings as part of their ministry.

We find the believers in Jerusalem praying for that power to continue even though it was beginning to bring them persecution:

> Now, Lord, consider their threats and enable your servants to speak your word with great boldness. Stretch out your hand to heal and perform miraculous signs and wonders through the name of your holy servant Jesus (Acts 4:29,30).

Wherever the gospel spread it was accompanied with power. Miracles were recorded in Iconium, Galatia, Philippi, and Ephesus, to name just a few places. And in Paul's writings to the believers at Corinth and Galatia he specifically encouraged them to expect this same power to work through their lives as well.

The early Christians were not excited over a new theology, but over the reality of Jesus' presence. He was alive among his people to share God's love and power, and they viewed miracles as one aspect of that power.

The Discrepancy

So where is that power today? Though many people can give accounts of God's healing or miraculous intervention in their lives, such occasions seem sporadic at best. And for every story of someone being healed it seems that there are so many more of people who are not.

Even in segments of the church that expect God to intervene regularly, the problems are many and the results are not outstanding. One well-known charismatic pastor admitted to me, "Statistically, healings in American ministries today don't even reach the placebo effect, those who are expected to get better just because they think they will. We don't even believe it ourselves."

Furthermore, where we do hear of healings today, not all the testimonies pan out. Dave Hunt cites a major healing ministry in the Los Angeles area where 80 people in the course of a service testified to miraculous healings. When a staff member did some follow-up on those people he found that not one of them had actually been healed.[3] Some people may have faked it while others must have experienced some temporary psychosomatic relief in the emotion of the moment.

Tim Stafford summed up well the disparity between the early church's experience and our own:

> While the Gospels and Acts are studded with the supernatural, accounts of the church since the second century are at best sporadically miraculous. Miracles could hardly be called the everyday experience of the church.[4]

Few would disagree with that statement, though the conclusions drawn from it can differ widely.

Some say that God's purpose for miracles in the New Testament was only to validate the authority of God's Word. They see miracles not as an act of God's compassion for hurting people but a mere validation stamp and therefore not necessary today. I have a hard time with that. What a cruel trick for God to show us in New Testament times what he can do to meet people's needs but refuse to do so now because we already have the Bible!

Many others affirm God's ability to miraculously intervene today, but feel that it is a rare act of sovereignty which leaves us little basis to expect healing in any given situation.

Still others suggest that God wants to heal every sickness in every person, and that people remain unhealed only because of sin or weak faith, or perhaps because they haven't taken the right steps.

All of these options leave me uncomfortable. Though I've witnessed many healings and outright miracles, I can honestly say that they don't seem to happen consistently enough and in as many specific situations as Scripture would seem to indicate they should. But I consider this a reason to look for change and not to discount God's intentions.

I am far more comfortable basing my expectations on the example of the early church than I am accommodating them to fit today's circumstances. Nowhere does the Bible intimate that miracles would cease after the first generation. That interpretation seems to begin where people try to rationalize their own experience. In fact, Scripture directly encourages us to anticipate God's pragmatic intervention in our lives—transforming, guiding, and even healing.

I know others disagree, but I'm convinced that the reason we do not experience God's power in greater measure than we do is for all the reasons this book contains. I don't think the church as a whole has lived to its potential since the first century, but not doing so and not being *able* to do so are two different things.

Though we want to see the church as a consistently faithful structure which only occasionally runs into problems, the opposite is more accurate. For the most part the church has floundered in its ineffectiveness, losing sight of Jesus' priorities for political, material, or personal gain. Perhaps when everything is said and done we'll see that we have not differed at all from Israel under the old covenant, where periods of forsaking God were only occasionally interrupted by the likes of Moses, Samuel, David, Jehoshaphat, and Daniel.

Today the worldliness that has filled our Christian institutions and reshaped our priorities could easily have robbed us of spiritual power. But if we can see that and turn from it, perhaps we can be on the verge of another interruption. Like Israel, the church has also had times of significant awakening and reformation that have called the church back to its biblical roots. Most of such times were accompanied by demonstrations of supernatural power in a variety of forms. Even today testimonies of God's miracle-working power dominate stories from overseas.

And at home signs and wonders are taking a more prominent place in theological discussions. The charismatic and Pentecostal movements have encouraged this for years, and now Peter Wagner and others are speaking of a "third wave" of renewal in this century, this time focusing on the release of God's power in miracles and healing outside of traditional charismatic settings.

But we must guard against the dangers of promoting any one aspect of the gospel, for this can easily lead to experiential extremes or institutional structures that may subvert and discredit what is biblically authentic. We must always ensure that the Giver is greater in our hearts than his gifts.

Miracles and healings are certainly not God's most important work in us, but their lack is more evident than other virtues which are more easily faked. If we can accept the New Testament example as valid today, it can be a great source of hunger that will call us to God's presence with a desire to be made better vessels for him. That hunger should not demand that every need be answered according to our expectations, nor should it question the faithfulness of those who are not healed.

Likewise that hunger need not discredit the ministries of those who have gone before us who haven't utilized such gifts. J. I. Packer poses a question which many people ask when contemplating miracles today: "In saying 'power' evangelism is normative, do they realize they are saying that the evangelism of John Wesley, D. L. Moody, Billy Sunday, and Billy Graham are sub-biblical?"[5]

Though it may have been demonstrated more in spiritual conviction than in healing, there is no doubt that these men exercised tremendous spiritual power. Not all power is measured by outward miracles. God uses our changed character and our selfless acts of giving as well as our convicting words to reach out to those who do not know him.

But neither for that reason should we discount God's desire to use a full arsenal through his church. Do we despise the soldier who takes a hill with just his bayonet because his gun jammed? Must we take every hill that way from now on to make him a hero?

Does God Want to Heal Everybody?

This question is asked whenever God's supernatural power is discussed. To answer the question accurately we need to take a wider look at God's use of supernatural power. It can be summed up in this statement: God is still active in his creation, not for man's amusement or entertainment, but for his redemption.

We need to see supernatural power in that light. Certainly it is most obvious in healings and miracles, but his activities are no less miraculous when he saves a life, fills a distressed heart with peace, or gives us the grace to endure difficulties. Some who miss that point try to force us into choosing between a God who works within and one who works without.

> There are many of us for whom the role model is Joni Eareckson rather than John Wimber. We see the powers of the kingdom operating, but mainly in regeneration, sanctification, the Spirit as a Comforter, the transformation of the inner life, rather than in physical miracles which just by happening prevent much of the other kingdom activity whereby people learn to live with their difficulties and glorify God.[6]

Eareckson is a quadriplegic who teaches on how to cope with suffering and has even shared her own frustrated efforts to find divine healing. Both Wimber and Eareckson have valuable ministries, but why should either be stereotyped and set up as a pattern for every person's life?

God wants to make us whole people in every area. The Word makes it clear that God's greatest concern for us is to transform us into his image. While this doesn't exclude physical healing, it does set God's priority. Those who seek God more extensively for healing than they do for freedom from sin aren't sharing God's desires, and probably not his power either.

I love my daughter deeply and will save her from whatever suffering I can, but I won't do so to the destruction of her inner maturity. So while I will get a sliver out of her finger before it gets infected, I won't seek the expulsion of a classmate who makes fun of her at school. I want her to grow up, and she needs to understand that suffering is part of that process in a godless world, even if we're believers.

That's what God does with us. He doesn't create our sufferings, but he is not bent on saving us from every little discomfort, either. Only a materialistic gospel forces us to make such an assumption.

But those who confine God's work to the nonphysical realm also cheat themselves. Outward miracles and divine healing both have a place in helping us to obey God's will, in attesting to his reality, and in demonstrating his love. God didn't just wind up his world and walk away from it. He is still active within it, able to affect the material realm as simply as he created it.

Two motives affect his use of power. First, gifts of healing—physical, spiritual, and emotional—are part of his work to reverse the devastation that sin and darkness have perpetrated on his children.

Second, miracles occur when God suspends the order of creation to advance his will. They simply attest to the fact that he who created is able to override that creation when it suits his purposes. For example, God created water to feed our crops and replenish our bodies' fluids. Of necessity it needed to be a liquid, and he supplies it to us through rain clouds. For the most part this serves his purposes; he doesn't need people walking on it, changing it into wine, or stopping storms.

Even though Jesus did all of these things once, he didn't take regular strolls across the Sea of Galilee or stop every storm that rolled over Judea. Even though he indicated that his disciples could expect to see God's power work on their behalf in the same way, there is no recorded case of them ever walking on water again or rebuking a storm to save a church picnic.

They learned their lesson. Miracles are designed to advance God's will, not satisfy our whims. Jesus was given the opportunity to use God's power for his own convenience when he was tempted to turn stones into bread. He declined. Miracles were never intended to save us from all discomforts but to give us what we need to follow Christ and be shaped into his likeness.

So does God want to heal everyone? Yes, both inside and outside—a process that will only be completed when we see him face-to-face. At each moment of our lives he knows the best way to change our lives. Either way, we need his power working in us to do it.

Though I look to affirm God's power however he chooses to manifest it, I believe there is a great lack today in outward miracles. I'm personally convinced that God wants to do more in this area than we presently experience today. Paul said, "My message and my preaching were not with wise and persuasive words, but in a demonstration of the Spirit's power, so that your faith might not rest on men's wisdom but on God's power" (1 Corinthians 2:4,5).

Does God want faith today based on anything less than this? We would do well to spend less time, effort, and money on apologetics and instead turn our resources to recovering the simplicity of yielding to God's power.

Let's Get On with It

Such recovery will be impossible if we don't see God's active participation in our lives as essential to our transformation and the extension of the gospel. We'll never pay the price necessary to find out how to let him work through us.

We've got to stop making excuses for ourselves and God, allowing us to coexist with the status quo instead of looking for change. By doing so we are like the naked emperor, who pretended that nonexistent clothing was good enough because at the moment that's all he had.

The other day as I walked across the campus of our local college I passed a young woman in a wheelchair. She was surrounded by her friends and was busily chatting away. My mind was drawn to Acts 3, of Peter and John and a lame man they sent home dancing.

How much would healing have said to this girl about God's love? What door would it have opened to those nearby to show them how real Jesus is? I do know one thing: I couldn't organize a more effective outreach than that one moment of spontaneity would produce.

I didn't do anything that day, but one day I shall—not for everyone I pass in a wheelchair, but for the ones God tells me to help. That's what Jesus is doing about suffering in our world: He isn't standing idly by while people hurt; he wants to intervene in the world's pain and bring redemption and salvation from the ravages of sin.

He showed us that fact when he was here, and he wants his gospel to still have that authority today—binding up broken hearts, healing blind eyes, delivering people out of darkness. All he awaits are vessels that will cooperate with him.

18

Clothed with Power

RESTORING SUPERNATURAL POWER

I tell you the truth,
anyone who has faith in me
will do what I have been doing.
He will do even greater things than these
because I am going to the Father.
And I will do whatever you ask in my name.
—John 14:12,13

"Reverend Jacobsen, this is the emergency room at Kaweah-Delta Hospital. There's been an accident involving some people from your congregation. Could you come down here right away?"

Even beneath the nurse's professionalism flowed an unmistakable current of urgency. I phoned Mark, my copastor, and left immediately. As I drove I began to seek God in prayer. Only then did I realize how little I knew about the situation into which I was headed. Who was it? What kind of accident?

The Spirit of God knew better than I, so I let him do the praying for me as I just opened my heart to God's presence. I was almost there when the thought raced across my mind: "I want that child to live." What child? Was that God?

After I identified myself to the emergency-room nurse, she led me past the suffering-filled rooms to a young couple standing in a busy corridor. Fear and despair filled their faces. Behind them in an examination room lay their only child, not even two years old. The sheets around his head were crimson with blood.

Through their weeping they pieced together the circumstances for me. Their son had been playing outside near the shoulder of their quiet residential street. A Jeep had inadvertently strayed off the road onto the shoulder, running over Jeffrey's head and crushing his skull.

The doctor confirmed what anyone could sense in the air—death was imminent. Mark, my copastor, arrived and we prayed in the hall, asking God to heal Jeffrey. When we were done the father wanted to go outside and collect his thoughts. He asked me to accompany him.

As we came to a busy intersection God spoke to me: "Have the father pray for his son right now." My heart was pounding. "Jeff, I feel that God wants you to pray for Jeffrey right now." On one of Visalia's busiest street corners we held hands and prayed. It was short but powerful, and tension gave way to peace. We hurried back to the emergency room.

Jeffrey still lay in the examining room as people scurried about him. "What's going on?" I asked Mark.

"Just a minute or so ago Jeffrey almost died. He went into arrest and the medical people thought it was over. Then all of a sudden he revived. They're taking him up now for surgery."

Even though the situation was still critical and the doctors told us that Jeffrey's chances were very slim, we were convinced that something had changed. The spirit of death was gone. During his quick recovery we continued to bathe him in prayer that the brain damage the doctors said was likely would never materialize. It didn't.

Though the miracle here was neither immediate nor indisputably verifiable medically, no one who was involved doubted God's intervention. As much as it testifies to God's working, however, it raises another question: Why could God show us to pray on that street corner in order to save Jeffrey from death, but not heal his skull completely?

Why Not Today?

Let me admit at the outset of this chapter that my hunger in the area of supernatural power far exceeds my experience. Though I've been fortunate to be a witness and beneficiary of many indisputable miracles, I'm presently involved in needs for healing, both physical and emotional, that have not yet been fulfilled despite intense prayer.

Many people take that as reason enough to question the availability of God's power today. I don't. The church today, captive to all the distractions we've talked about in this book, is not living in biblical normality. We are not as full of God's power as we should be. Prayers go unanswered not because God has changed his plan but because we haven't learned how to let his power flow through us.

We are a generation mostly won to Christ through the persuasion of orators, not the power of God's presence. Paul warned us that such people would have the inclination to put their trust in man's wisdom instead of God's power. And that we do. Our models of success are found in spellbinding personalities, diligent planning, or good old-fashioned hard work. Many believers have never witnessed an outright miracle, and consequently they think of prayer as nothing more than the pronouncement of blessing on their own efforts.

To make matters worse, many who talk of God's power being used today discredit that theology with financial abuse, immorality, egotism, and false claims of success. Some are charlatans who try to fake God's power for their own gain. Many others may be well-intentioned but haven't learned the difference between an emotional frenzy and the Holy Spirit.

We also face the disappointments of our own past unanswered prayers. Even when we were the most sure that our requests were not selfish, and we sought God with all our heart, our prayers were powerless to change the circumstances. To pray in expectancy again we need to get past these disappointments.

Certainly these problems make it difficult to flow with God's power, but not impossible. The evidence of Scripture must outweigh any lack of evidence we find in our own experience. God does want us to participate in his power, and we can find it again if we will mine the depths of his presence like a prospector after gold.

Learning to be vessels of God's power does not come naturally for any of us. We cannot expect to walk in spiritual reality with the same methods we use in the material realm. That's like trying to use the same rules underwater that we do on land. They just don't work.

We learn to navigate on land even before we can remember, and doing so becomes second nature. But put us underwater and everything changes. Instead of gravity forcing us down, buoyancy pulls us up. Speech is unintelligible underwater, and breathing itself becomes a calculated activity. Walking is a nearly fruitless endeavor and running is impossible. To move effectively in water you have to learn to swim.

In the same way, our life in the material world leaves us unprepared for the supernatural. Though being born of the Spirit opens us to the reality of the spiritual world, we must still learn to move in it. Seeing how it works will not only give us direction for how we can change but will show us why some of our past expectations have not been met.

God's Power

Here are six characteristics that will help us gain an understanding of how God's power can flow more effectively in our life.

1. *God's power cherishes intimacy above activity.* Life in the material world prefers achievement to relationships, and so it is natural for us to prefer doing things for God instead of letting him work through us.

Jesus taught us another way: "If you remain in me . . . ask whatever you wish, and it will be given you" (John 15:7). God's power flows only out of intimacy. All the seminars, techniques, and outlines in the world won't replace that reality. Loving and obeying God is all that is necessary to his working in us.

"Does God give you his Spirit and work miracles among you because you observe the law, or because you believe what you heard?" (Galatians 3:5). Miracles happen not because we've learned to obey all the right rules but because we believe God.

Throughout this book we've dealt with the many elements in Christianity today that distract people from intimacy. Those distractions exact a price—the power of God's life. For the most part Christians today live fragmented and disjointed lives, seduced as much by the busyness of the church as the pleasures of this world. Hudson Taylor drives the point home:

"An easygoing, non-self-denying life will never be one of power."[1]

We kid ourselves if we think we can move in God's power without effectively relating to him every day in worship, prayer, and Bible study. That's where he purifies us, equips us, and fills us with his presence so that we don't have to live our lives out of our own resources. If we won't come there we shouldn't complain when our prayers don't move God to action.

That is where faith is nurtured, and over and over again Scripture tells us that God's working hinges on our faith. Our old nature says, "I'll believe it when I see it," but the Word calls us to "live by faith, not by sight" (2 Corinthians 5:7). The primary realities of this universe are not observed by physical senses. God's presence works at a far deeper level than eyes, ears, and rationalism can touch. Faith is our link to what is unseen, helping us to see God's will and giving us the strength to obey it.

Faith today is sorely misunderstood by those who think it to be a spiritual force they can use to fulfill their own pleasures. They are always trying to prove faith by positive confessions (which often end up to be outright lies) and by token acts. But nothing could be more futile. Faith describes our entire relationship with God, one that is based on trust, sensitivity, and submission to his will.

Not only does God's power flow through our relationship with him, but it is also the conduit that lets us share that power with others. Often when Jesus healed people he was moved with compassion. What moves us when we pray for others? I know I'm often bombarded with an awareness of how bad I'm going to look if nothing happens. God's power doesn't move freely in that environment.

At other times I've prayed for a miracle specifically to avoid more costly personal involvement. My prayer was not an extension of my compassion but a substitute for it, like asking God to heal the beaten man on the road in the parable of the Good Samaritan because this would be easier than bandaging the wounds and paying for his stay at an inn. The early church regarded selling their property to help one another in financial need as a miracle just as real as multiplying the loaves and fishes. Until we're moved enough to spend our resources, chances are we're not ready to rely on God's.

Our own intimate relationship to God is the well out of which spiritual power flows. Without it, all our efforts and petitions will never come to pass.

2. *God's power is all-inclusive.* God's power cannot be selectively received. That explains why many people pray for godly things, only to be disappointed when they don't happen. We can't limit God's working to just one area of our lives. Unless we are as concerned for God to heal us of our sin and selfish ambitions as we are our diseases, we cannot expect him to just be there when we want him.

"Do not pray for the well-being of this people. Although they fast, I will not listen to their cry. . . . I will not accept them. Instead, I will destroy them with the sword, famine and plague" (Jeremiah 14:11,12). For years the Israelites had served their own pleasures, ignoring God's warnings. Now in their crisis they wanted him to make everything better. But God told Jeremiah that no amount of prayer would now summon his action.

God is not a genie whom we can call out of a bottle to help further our selfishness. When we invite him to work in our behalf, he comes to every area of our lives to make us like himself. Those who want to restrict him to their own personal comfort really misunderstand just what kind of God he is. It is a subtle rebellion, to be sure, but one that still denies us his power.

That's why it is ridiculous for us to ask if God wants to heal everyone. Certainly he is a healing God, but there are times when God looks past our temporal circumstances to heal the greater diseases of selfishness and sin in our lives. As with surgery, some healing comes only through further pain.

3. *God's power is released by his activity, not his ability.* God can do anything. His power over creation is total and complete. He

could turn this book into a piece of chocolate cake, but I doubt that he'll do it no matter how badly you might want him to.

Faith doesn't rest on what God *can* do but on what he *will* do. Abraham was commended for his faith, not for the son *he wanted*, but for the son *God had promised*: "[He was] fully persuaded that God had the power to do what he had promised" (Romans 4:21).

That's why intimacy is the link to God's power. Until we see what God is doing in a given situation, we have no basis to be confident about its outcome. Jesus himself lived that way: "I tell you the truth, the Son can do nothing by himself; he can do only what he sees his Father doing, because whatever the Father does the Son also does" (John 5:19). God wants us as well to know what he's doing, so we can cooperate with him. Listen to him when you pray. He will show you, and then you can proceed with confidence.

Generalized promises won't suffice in this setting, nor will our own conclusions about what we think is best. God's work is too personal for such questions, and his wisdom too great. He considers more variables than we could ever hope to comprehend, picking the best of all possible answers. And, as we said in the last chapter, his greatest priority will not be providing for our personal comfort but transforming us into his image.

4. God's power flows through obedient people. You cannot read the Bible and find support for the idea that God will do his work regardless of how people respond to him. Ephesians 3:20 says, "To him who is able to do immeasurably more than all we ask or imagine, according to his power that is at work within us." The New Testament is an appeal for vessels, people through whom God's power can work, to bring his will into the reality of human experience.

One of the greatest deterrents to people growing in their use of spiritual power is the attitude that no matter what we do, God's work will still be accomplished. Such thinking is only thinly veiled fatalism. People who believe this are the ones who blame God for babies born deformed or a young father dying in a car crash. But God is not responsible for either of these.

In an otherwise-excellent book on God's nature, *The Auto-biography of God*, Lloyd John Ogilvie falls into a trap that keeps many believers from seeking God wholeheartedly: "If God wants it, no one can stop it. If he doesn't there's no way you can pull it off anyway. So relax."[2]

Though I agree with Ogilvie that human effort cannot perform God's work, I cannot agree that everything in this age conforms to God's will so easily. "The whole world is under the control of the evil one" (1 John 5:19). Satan is the cause of the anguish of this world, and yet one of his greatest deceits has been to get people to blame God for it. He is not greater than God in moving history toward his defeat at the second coming of Christ. Until then Satan is the ruler of those who belong to this age, and through them he seeks to destroy the work of God.

Through us God wants to prevail over him, but this does not mean that we win every battle. About his attempts to get to Thessalonica, Paul said that Satan thwarted him three times. He didn't say that it wasn't God's will—only that he had lost a battle.

5. *God's power is simple.* Part of the reason it is difficult for us to flow with God's power is that we are so awed by it. We don't see how simple it is for God to heal cancer or emotional scars, so we are overwhelmed by it all. We can't imagine God working through us in power, so consequently we don't let him.

Jesus tried to drive home that point to his disciples on one occasion. After miraculously satisfying the hunger of 5000 people with only five loaves of bread and two fish, Jesus sent his disciples across the lake. In the middle of the night he came to them in the midst of a storm—walking on the lake! They were terrified as he walked up to them and climbed into the boat. Immediately the storm ceased. In Mark 6:51,52 we read, "They were completely amazed, for they had not understood about the loaves."

What about the loaves? Jesus was showing them how easy it is for God to change the natural world. He didn't want them to be awed by God's power, because he wanted them to *use* that power, and he knew they would never do so as long as they were so amazed by it. If that was true for them, it will be much more difficult for us.

They lived at a time when almost everyone accepted the fact that unseen forces controlled the actions of matter. Even the heathen feared that the dimming of the sun during an eclipse resulted from angry gods. Now we know that such is not the case. An eclipse is merely the result of the moon's predictable orbit crossing between earth and sun. For them an eclipse was a terrifying surprise, but we can pinpoint the exact time and location of any future occurrence.

For them to believe that devils inhabited people, that water could be made into wine, or that a lame person could be instantaneously healed by Peter's shadow falling across him was not as great a jump as it is for us. We "know" why people are sick; we can diagnose it medically and even prescribe treatment with statistical odds for its effectiveness.

For us to imagine God intervening in that process is staggering, and is probably our greatest deterrent to the miraculous. Scripture clearly says that our expectancy is a major ingredient in cooperating with God's power. We need to return to the childlike affirmation that our God is big enough to do whatever he wants to in his creation.

6. *God's power is practical.* It is not some mysterious unobservable force. One day a woman touched Jesus' cloak as he passed through a crowd; she sought to be healed of incurable bleeding. The moment she touched him she was healed, and Jesus whirled around to find out who touched him. The disciples were confused by the question because the entire crowd was pressing against him. "Someone touched me; I know that power has gone out from me" (Luke 8:46).

Jesus knew when God's power was at work. He said we could expect that same power to flow out of our lives: "Whoever believes in me . . . streams of living water will flow from within him" (John 7:38). That's the essence of power. It is not our words or our actions, but the flow of God's Spirit rising out of us to touch others.

I've prayed for people possessed by demons, saying all the right words with tremendous authority in my voice, but seen nothing happen. At other times I've just quietly worshiped God as that flow of life poured out of my being and shattered the powers of darkness.

Once you've had some experience with it, you'll be able to tell when God is moving through your prayers and when he is not. When he's not, stop for a moment and reexamine the situation. Are you following what God wants to do? Does he have something else to reveal? Ministering God's life is not playing some mystery game. We can know what's going on and can cooperate with him.

A Lesson from the Trenches

The best training ground for moving in God's power is not in the sanctuary but in the street. For too long the gifts of the Spirit have been used like toys in the nursery instead of weapons in battle. You don't learn to move in the supernatural at seminars—you learn by doing. That's where Jesus put his disciples. Let's look at one of those instances and what Jesus taught his disciples about growing in his power.

Mark 9:14-29 tells the story of a young, demon-possessed boy tormented by seizures. The disciples had already prayed for him unsuccessfully when his father brought him to Jesus. When the demon saw Jesus, he threw the boy into a convulsion. He fell to the ground frothing at the mouth. Jesus calmly questioned the father for a few moments, getting the facts and challenging him to believe in God. As a crowd began to gather Jesus rebuked the demon, causing it to shriek, shake the boy violently, and finally depart. The boy lay motionless. Many thought he was dead, but Jesus took him by the hand and lifted him up.

What can we learn from this encounter?

1. *Get involved with people in need.* People who say the church doesn't need a miracle today aren't spending time with anyone who really needs one. When you see the need in light of God's Word you won't be able to hang back. The disciples at

least tried, even if unsuccessfully. Only people who try fail, and if we're humble in failure God can even turn around failures for his glory.

One pastor I know tells of praying for the sick for ten months before he ever saw someone healed in his church. Only people with that kind of determination are going to learn how to be effective.

2. *Be convinced of God's objective.* After the disciples failed, the father took his son to Jesus. Jesus reaffirmed God's desire, and they got back to the battle. Too many people assume that their failed efforts are an indication that God must have a different objective.

Seek God until you understand what he wants to do and how he wants it done. That's information which his Spirit wants to give you.

3. *Get the facts*, from the situation and from the Spirit. From the father Jesus found out about the boy's condition and built faith in the father. Was it during this time that Jesus looked to see what the father was doing? I think so, for he never approached needs in exactly the same way. He treated each person as an individual.

Some were healed on the spot, others later; some by a word, others by washing spit out of their eye. I'm convinced that the differences in form were more than just God's desire for variety. Jesus was ministering at a level far deeper than people's physical need, and how he met that need advanced his work in other areas of their life as well.

4. As long as you're convinced of God's desire, *stay with the need.* This is probably where the disciples let down. If the boy was flung into convulsions when they started to pray, they probably thought their prayers were only making matters worse, so they stopped. Could this be what Jesus referred to when he said that this kind comes out only by much prayer? Prayer must continue until God's will is carried out. How often the Word challenges us to persevere, particularly as it relates to prayer!

We cannot expect the enemy to give in so easily, especially when God reveals his will. He is a thief and will always try to steal God's power.

To learn perseverance we must stop seeing our prayers as requisition forms laid on the desk of a supervisor. If that's all prayer is, there is no reason to give God more than one prayer to act on. True prayer is the vehicle by which God brings his power into our circumstances. Our perseverance challenges whatever resists God's will in us or in the circumstance. That's why many of the prayers for miracles in the Bible are directed at the sickness, storm, or demon: "Be healed. Be still. Be gone." Perseverance doesn't wear God down with our requests; it wears down the resistance to him in our world.

How long should you persevere? Until you're convinced that the outcome matches God's desire. We prayed with one demon-plagued young lady over a five-month period until she was free. There are healing needs in our fellowship today that we're still praying for. By and large, however, all-night marathon sessions don't prove very effective. If there doesn't seem to be clear direction as to how God is moving, retreat to some times of prayer and fasting so that he can give further wisdom. Then come back to the need later.

5. Finally, *learn from your efforts*. The disciples did that. They came to Jesus afterward and asked, "Why couldn't we drive it out?" That's why it is always best to pray with a team (two or three) who can then discuss the results later. Let God show you what you did right and where you missed him, so that you can be more effective in the future. Include some inexperienced people among you so they don't have to stay that way.

God wants to take the mystery out of his supernatural power so that he can use you to advance his will in our age. Let him teach you how.

His Presence
in Every Circumstance

19

Stained Glass and White Linen

THE LOSS OF RELEVANCE

Their cobwebs are useless for clothing;
they cannot cover themselves with what they make.
—Isaiah 59:6

I sat just behind three of them, but the room was full of many others. They were in their early twenties and had come in anguish to a funeral of one of their friends who had been killed in a tragic accident. He and his family were dedicated believers, but it was obvious by the conversation in front of me that these were not.

The ever-present organ music masked the grieving silence. Though unspoken, one question reverberated in that room: "Why?" It was most detectable among the non-Christians. Their icy stares challenged the church for answers to the question "If there is a God, why this?"

The service began with the congregation singing "God Is So Good." The only reference to the death came in a brief welcome from the pastor to what he called a coronation, not a funeral. Then we got a three-point sermon on why someone should give his heart to God. The words of that service never rose to meet the agony of the people, the seeming incongruity between God's love and sudden tragedy.

I watched with interest these three in front of me. Often during the service they glanced at each other, always conveying the same thing. Either by a roll of the eyes, a smirked grimace, or a shaking of the head in disgust they were appalled that the church in the midst of such pain would stick its head in the sand and pretend that this is a great blessing. It didn't even try to deal with the pain in the room, and probably not because it didn't want to but because it didn't know how to address the questions.

221

I have no doubt that those young people left the room more hardened to God's love. Their short-term concern was with his relevance to this tragedy, but they didn't find him relevant, and they were sure that even the believers there hadn't either. Death was portrayed as God's friend, working for some higher purpose, when the Word already makes it clear that death is his enemy as well as ours. Neither his wisdom nor his love was brought to bear on the anguish in that room.

The larger question, however, is whether Jesus is relevant to anything in our lives. Os Guiness reiterates that indictment: "The damning comment has been made of Christianity that it is privately engaging but socially irrelevant."[1]

Until the church can answer the difficult questions that emerge from the application of our theology into real human experience, the world will only sit back and laugh. To them our gospel is irrelevant, a placebo designed to set the ignorant at ease and not a real answer for desperate needs.

In the fictional novel *Codename: Sebastian* a young pastor faces this problem in graphic fashion. With a small band of survivors Sebastian is wandering, thirsty and near death, in the unbearable heat of the Negev. His pain overwhelms the depth of his Christian experience, and he asks God if he is even in such places. "If you're not I don't blame you. You belong in cathedrals with high altars and communion tables wrapped in white linen . . . not here, not in this valley of death."[2]

The story may be fictional, but the cry is not. How quickly the serenity we feel in our sanctuaries evaporates in the confusion and pain of this world! It is not meant to be so. Jesus has real answers for real people in real situations. He does not want to only exist in Sunday services, but also in unemployment lines, cancer wards, and those lonely moments of doubt and despair. Here is yet another sign of our nakedness, and another opportunity to find the joy of intimacy.

Church-Produced Hypocrites

One would have to be blind not to see the great disparity between what the church teaches on Sunday morning and what Christians live out during the week. It is seen so clearly in the way people conduct business, treat their children, choose their entertainment, or relate to people around them. Of such people the charge of *hypocrite* is raised, and everyone knows the church is full of them.

Such a term fits those who only pretend to serve God. The mockery they make of God should not be tolerated, regardless of how much money they give. They only milk the church to their own advantage. But there is another problem here: people who genuinely want to follow God but find themselves unable to do so.

There are a lot of people in this category. Year after year they come weeping to the altar, confessing that the life they are living is not the one they desire. They promise to be different, only to find themselves a few months later entangled again in the distractions of Western living, unequipped to make the work of Jesus real in their lives. They may be bound by sin or broken by the enemy's hand, but somehow the message escapes them. What seems so powerful on Sunday morning fizzles in their home and on the job.

This irrelevance in Christian experience does not result so much from hardened hearts as from our packaging of Christianity that has separated it from real human experience.

Look at our settings for worship. How real are they? For one hour on Sundays we meet in color-coordinated serenity, designed at great expense to invoke worship and peacefulness through the use of vaulted ceilings, warm carpeting, and homey wall coverings. Our children are conveniently hidden in the bowels of the building. Placid organ music, melodious anthems, and eloquent oratory create a controlled atmosphere for ministry.

Contrast that with life during the rest of the week, surrounded by four walls that continually grow closer together. Children bicker, always needing something—a toy fixed, a problem solved. The only background music to be heard are the choruses of anxiety and the strains of a busy schedule. No wonder people lament, "I try to touch God at home, but he's not there like he is at church." Rather than pat ourselves on the back, we ought to repent that we're not teaching people how to find God's presence away from our plastic (or Plexiglas) settings.

Look at church people. They aren't real either. They dress in their Sunday finest, both in clothes and in attitude—plastic people in pewed rows. No one shares their failures or needs. Those paraded in front are successful in the eyes of the world: musicians, beauty queens, athletes, business people. Oddly, no one seems to be having fun, and when it's all over they file back out to the jaws of a waiting world.

Contrast that with a world where people scrape to find a meal, where frustrated parents yell at their children, where sin tears at their life to destroy them. Such problems aren't brought to church because people have found the church unable to help them. People's weaknesses are too often only a source of gossip and stereotyping. Real questions go unasked because the risk of being thought a doubter is too great. Too often it is true that the world treats its own with more compassion than the church does.

Look at our leaders. Are they real people? They speak in deeper-than-average tones and deliver sermons with high-pitched fever and four-bit words for which they would get laughed off the street in the real world. Greek exegesis, intricate outlines, and well-turned phrases are used more to impress people than to teach them something they can understand.

Even something as seemingly unimportant as dress enhances this separation. Liturgical robes, academic gowns, and even three-piece suits can be used to garner a false sense of authority. Even earthly rulers gave up wearing robes and miters hundreds of years ago. Jesus didn't seek authority through his clothing. He was trying to show people that a real life with God was available to *them*, and was not reserved for someone professionally trained and ornately attired.

This was brought graphically home to me one summer Sunday morning. The temperature was in the high 90's and climbing. I was already soaking with sweat in my three-piece navy suit as I greeted those gathering for service. I hadn't noticed that they were all in short-sleeved sport shirts until a friend leaned over to me and with as much gentleness as possible said, "You really don't know how ridiculous you look in that suit, do you?"

Our current emphasis on celebrity leadership only compounds the problem. They drop names of the famous they've been with and their jet-setting schedule. An entourage meets their every need, and the only people they see stare at them in awe of their greatness. When was the last time someone talked to them honestly or they tried to help someone pregnant, unmarried, angry at God, and rejected by everyone around them? It's a shock that so many people listen to such leaders and no wonder to me that the world doesn't.

What connection does our program have with the real world? Anything significant is done by a professional, in a closed forum after days of preparation. How does that prepare people to meet the world head-on, where people interrupt with real and difficult questions, where merely saying "because the Bible says so" isn't enough?

We don't offer real answers to the questions, doubts, and fears that people face. Pat answers and formulas substitute for God's presence and intervention. "Something good is going to happen to you" does little for the couple blaming God for the death of their baby. "The family that prays together stays together" does nothing for the wife who has just found out that her husband, the deacon, has just been caught in someone else's bed. "You just need to trust God more" may be true, but unless we help people actually do this, such a statement only causes greater guilt.

Don't think I'm exaggerating the impact of Sunday services. It is always a church's largest gathering, and rare is the church that touches any more than half of those people again at other weekly functions. I know that many people in the Sunday-morning crowd are only looking for a religious token, but there are also many who have been shut out by the church's irrelevance.

They've been convinced of their incompetence in living a fulfilling walk with Jesus outside the church's walls. They are isolated. Their perception of God failing them is only exceeded by the guilt they feel for failing him. One pastor told me he estimated that 90 percent of church people live with an underlying disappointment and anger directed at God.

This may be a source for the many hypocrites we decry. God fits on Sunday mornings but nowhere else. On the way out of the service they are already gossiping about each other, and perhaps by Monday they are once again trapped in sin. Many, like the Israelites, still take manna breaks even as they forge their golden calf.

The Greater Grief

The effects of irrelevance, however, aren't felt just in the church. Like the unknown trio sitting ahead of me at the funeral, such irrelevance alienates the world from God. To the world we have become what one writer termed "islands of irrelevance in a sea of despair."[3]

Not seeing us as any different for the relationship we claim to have with God, the world concludes that we have only fabricated him in our minds. Christianity is a crutch, they say; and who can blame them? We've already cited evidence that any statistic true of the general populace is largely true of the church as well.

They also see that we don't handle disappointment and crisis much better than they do either. In fact, Christians often weather crises worse, because in addition to their trial they are usually blaming God or the church for not helping them out of it. Recently I sat with an elderly saint whose body is wasting away. This woman had given much to the body of Christ, so I was taken back by her bitterness and hostility at God for not healing her or taking her home. The world fairly asks, "If it doesn't make any difference for you, why should I give it a try?"

I walked into a local auto repair shop recently that prominently displays the sign of a fish in all its advertisements.

Tracts cluttered the counter, but behind it the manager was on the phone. He was angry about some change in procedure regarding the church kitchen and was talking to another church member about it. In a loud voice that filled the entire room he lambasted with profanity the pastor and other members of the church. I cringed in embarrassment for that man and the church he was tearing apart. As I looked around the room others smirked, shaking their heads. What else do you expect from the church?

One episode like that speaks louder than 20 citywide crusades. It's not that the world is looking for perfection, but (reasonably so) they at least expect to see some evidence that in fact the God of the universe has taken up residence in us.

Here is the cost of the benign gospel we preach. We are happy to fill our churches even though we know that many people are coming for reasons other than to surrender their lives to God. Though we may know the difference, the world does not. The pseudo-Christians we protect are the greatest deterrent to more genuine people finding reality in Christ.

We don't even see the results of our best intentions. Not long ago I was invited to a public prayer meeting to intercede for someone dying with cancer. Friends and famiily were invited, including people who were not even believers. The pastor of this woman rose to pray. With a strong and confident voice he claimed her healing: "We know that tomorrow morning she'll walk out of that hospital healed." Waves of amens filled the room.

Within a month she died. The same pastor conducted the funeral with the same people present. With the same confidence that he had told them she would walk out well he told them that they could put their trust in God. Don't we see how ridiculous we look? The world is less amazed with the fact that she wasn't healed than with the fact that it didn't seem to make any difference to us that what we told them didn't come to pass.

To them the church looks like an ostrich, hiding its head in the sand while pretending all is well no matter what happens.

That's what is behind the charge of Christianity being a crutch. If by this charge the critics meant something to lean on that promotes healing, I would welcome that assessment of Christianity. But they mean that Christianity isn't real; it's only a figment of our imagination to help us ignore reality.

I can't imagine such a charge being leveled at James, Peter, or Paul. Their Christianity was no crutch. Their association with the gospel cost them daily. It was a source of persecution, not fame and fortune. Their joy came not in pretending that the real world didn't exist but in finding joy in spite of pain and hope in the midst of trials. People were changed and lives were touched; even those who didn't accept the church's message were still awed by its effectiveness.

Unless we rediscover that kind of gospel, our irrelevance will continue to build an impenetrable wall between us and the world. That's a problem the Pharisees faced as they hid in the safety of their own subculture. In the face of real needs they could only respond with rules of order and the condemnatory teaching that tragedy is the result of sin. We're building that same wall now, alienating the very people who hunger for what we're supposed to offer. But all we can find to offer is our creed: "Believe these things and life will go better."

Chuck Colson in his book *Loving God* writes about this growing wall and its devastating effects.

> When the church fails to break the barrier, both sides lose. Those who need the gospel of hope and the reality of love don't get it; and the isolated church keeps evangelizing the same people over and over until its only mission finally is to entertain itself.[4]

Without the challenge to make the gospel real in the arena of human need, our gospel degenerates into a toy for our own amusement. We beg the world to come see us and condemn them when they don't. Most evangelism is only offered in closed-forum settings. Come to our church, our crusade, our rally—places we control. Jesus never claimed his own turf. He didn't bring crowds into orchestrated services. Whether with Pharisee or harlot, he sat in their homes and spoke in their synagogues—and suffered retribution for doing so.

Colson continues:

> Isn't it interesting that Jesus didn't set up an office in the temple and wait for people to come to Him for counseling. Instead he went to them—to the homes of the most notorious sinners, to the places where he would most likely encounter the handicapped and sick, the needy, the outcasts of society.[5]

We are afraid to move out of the serenity of our own sanctuary. When we do it is only to shove a tract in someone's face, put a Scripture on a T-shirt and jump in front of an ABC Sports camera, circulate ready-made questionnaires or buy TV time. Again it's our forum, our terminology, our rules. The result is the same. They watch us, but we don't ever enter into their struggle with the personal touch of Jesus Christ to transform their life. Why? Because we're afraid. If Jesus hasn't been real for us, how can we make him real for them?

This is the greater grief. I'm saddened by people who haven't found the gospel powerful enough to transform them, but sadder still for others who have never come looking because they see no evidence of its reality.

Safety First

I hope you understand the story of the naked emperor better now than when you began this book, because we need to see that we are just like him. We don't want to be irrelevant any more than he wanted to parade naked before his city. We get tricked, however, when we are concerned about our own safety instead of being honest. Just a touch of honesty in any one of the emperor's entourage would have saved him from the most embarrassing consequences.

When it finally came, it was too late. Too much would be risked to change now. In the same way we are trapped when we love safety more than we love Jesus. The church has become its own safe subculture. Ritual and tradition mask our emptiness and pat answers our questions. Everyone knows his part and fulfills it without rocking the boat. We are in control, and though the boat may not be all that powerful, at least it is safe.

We don't have to face the difficult implications of the truths we espouse. Do we really believe that the people with whom we exchange such casual smiles throughout the day are really being deceived into destruction by Satan and his army? If we do, why can we pass them any more easily than we would an injured child on a playground? Instead, we immerse ourselves in our own entertainment so we don't have to see the casualties.

Whenever anyone cuts through the facade by getting serious about being a disciple of Jesus, we try to discourage him. By calling such people fanatics we can crawl back behind the compromises which their presence exposes.

Being relevant, however, calls us away from our safe havens. The gospel is not safe, neither for us who accept it nor for the world with whom we are to share it. It will challenge, stretch, and change us, all to his glory and our joy—but not without the violent resistance of our flesh.

The world reacts in much the same way, and that is the sign of a relevant gospel. It may not be welcomed with joy, but it at least won't be met with apathy. The reality of Jesus forces people to be exposed for what they are. It is a smell of death to those who are perishing and a scent of life to those who are being saved. Not everyone liked the early church's message, but at least the church commanded the respect of that entire society. Contrast that with the general disrepute which the church suffers today, not for its message but for its preoccupation with money and its condescending attitude.

The gospel will offend people, but the Bible challenges us to be sure that the offense comes only because of truth and not because we are personally offensive in our conduct or methods. But we distort the truth to make it palatable instead of letting Jesus change us so that our character will bear his image.

One year my wife and I went to the Tournament of Roses Parade in Pasadena. After the parade a group of people walked up the street with "Repent" signs as one of them lambasted the crowd through a megaphone: "What's the matter, Mr. Businessman? Are you too good for Jesus? You will burn in hell for your sins." Can you imagine Jesus doing that? I was embarrassed for every person there, especially the non-Christians.

If people are going to be offended, let it be with the lordship of Jesus, not our arrogance or extravagance. Jesus approached the world with compassion for all, even those rejecting him, but this doesn't mean that he emphasized forgiveness to the exclusion of challenging people to follow him.

In the third book of the science-fiction series *Dune*, the false religion of that society was blasted by a prophet from the wilderness. The same question could be put to us today: "You, priest . . . are a chaplain to the self-satisfied. . . . I come to challenge you. Is your religion real when it costs you nothing and carries no risk?"[6]

We cannot hide in the safety of our own irrelevant structures while a world dies around us. God has called us to go there, risking whatever danger we fear, to allow him to extend his reality through us.

> I do know we can come out of our safe sanctuaries and move alongside those in need and begin to demonstrate some caring concern. Our presence in a place of need is more powerful than a thousand sermons. *Being there* is our witness. And until we are, our orthodoxy and doctrine are mere words, our liturgies and gospel choruses ring hollow.[7]

The New Testament vibrates with a relevant God able to penetrate every situation. It was a gospel that fit where sickness and death hung heavy in the air, where people mingled at a wedding reception, where they pretended religion at a Pharisee's banquet, where little children could find a place on Jesus' lap, where a crazed man threatened people from the graveyard, and where God's people endured suffering and death at the hands of a cruel world.

God is not the God of stained glass and white linen. He can be there, of course, but he is also in unemployment lines and cancer wards, family birthday parties and vacation trips, inexplicable accidents and dark nights of doubt. Don't you want to find him there in the fullness of his reality? Don't you want to help others see how God comes to them in love and mercy?

20

A Real Jesus in an Unreal World

RESTORING RELEVANCE

As the Father has sent me,
I am sending you.
—John 20:21

Remember our poor friend Sebastian, the fictitious pastor marooned in the hot Negev by a plane crash? Well, his doubt and anger grew as their situation in the desert worsened. Finally a stewardess, seeing what a harmful effect he was having on the others, confronted him.

> You've got to prove to yourself that you are more than a Biblical Band-Aid panhandler. You've got to prove to yourself and this miserable bunch of suffering humanity that God exists in the proportion that you've been preaching most of your life from the sterile, antiseptic, safe pulpits.[1]

It is a challenge that we need to hear too, even though a naked church cringes from such a challenge, unsure that Christianity can survive in the cold reality of this world. The excuses are many. "Isn't it a bit too old-fashioned and confining?" "People are so focused on their own pleasure that they don't need a Savior." "How can I share with someone else what isn't even working for me?" "You try to walk a real Christianity in this world and you could get killed."

We've all heard and made those excuses and many more. Some of them are even right, especially the getting killed part. Many people already have, including our Founder and almost all of his first followers.

Can Christianity make it in today's world? We can almost talk ourselves out of that one, but is it really the right question?

Aren't we really asking whether God can make it in the real world? With the ambiguity out of the way it certainly is a ridiculous question.

Not only can God make it here, but it's the only place he does make it. He is not afraid to meet people in the real world, where every battle is not won, where people hurt and die, where all don't repent and are saved. He's not afraid of hospital rooms and screams of anger by people who misunderstand his love. He knows better than we that everything in this age will not end in temporal joy and that rarely are the righteous rewarded by this world.

He is not a God who can be real only in stained-glass hues on velvet pews. If that's the only place we're finding him, then we're not finding the God of Abraham, Isaac, and Jacob. What we're finding is an aesthetic feeling or a surge of compassion, but not the God of the universe filling our lives with the reality of his presence.

God only stays in a church building if that's where we leave him, and that's where many people prefer to have him. He's there when we need him, but he won't meddle in my business, my family, or my recreational time.

But this is written for those to whom God's presence is good news—those who want to know him more fully, not less so. As in the last section, this too is a growing edge for both me and the fellowship in which I pastor. We still talk about it better than we do it, but we're learning.

We've seen the conventional forms of citywide crusades, TV evangelists, and door-to-door visitations missing the mark. Even the best attempts produce few people who move on to the fullness of life in Christ. For all our efforts the level of spiritual life in the West declines rapidly, even among professing Christians. With far less sophisticated measures the church has grown profusely in such places as China and Africa. Though this fact does not necessarily negate our methods, it forces us to contemplate whether we should be putting all our efforts into them.

Broken people rarely seem to make it to our programmed settings, and neither do the hungry. They've sat through them before and found them lifeless. The only way to reach them is to go into their world and show them how much Jesus cares about them. But here lies the difficulty, for this age is built on lies and misconceptions. It prefers personal comfort to objective truth and self-sufficiency to dependence on God. But that is our task—to make Jesus real in a world that runs from reality.

Substance over Style

Just how do we present a relevant gospel to the world? Like everything else, there are right ways and wrong ways, and the wrong ones are easiest.

Some people seek to be relevant by becoming just like the world in speech, dress, and actions. Singing groups, only identifiable as Christian by the words on the record jacket, imitate their secular counterparts. TV evangelists invite the dubious testimonials of Hollywood luminaries whose own relationship to God is at best questionable. And closer to home, believers tell off-color jokes or join in the office gossip so unbelievers won't think they are prudes. But if we look just like the world, what will they find in us worth having?

Look down the street at the professed Christians on your block. What do you see different about their lives that shows the world that Jesus lives in them? And don't say they go to church, because that's not the point. People who go to church just to find some peace are already churchgoers. The rest want to see if going to church changes anything. If it doesn't, and they see us pursuing the same objectives as the world, they won't see any sense in Christianity, and I don't blame them.

Imitating the world is often only an excuse to join it. And once you've done that, you've got nothing left to offer it.

Other people take the opposite extreme. Cloistering in their own subculture with dress, songs, and terminology from past decades or even centuries, they seek relevance by presenting a conspicuous alternative to the world. Such subcultures survive through legalism, and legalism can only measure outward nonessentials. The world is not interested. This attempt at relevance is an escape from the difficult challenge of having to live in the changing realities of the world without succumbing to worldliness.

Still others distort the gospel to fit worldly desires. Find out what the world wants and give it to them in Christian terms. To entertain them we turn the church into variety shows, hoping that entertainment will substitute for truth. To satiate pride and egotism we teach a gospel of self-esteem and self-works. To appease the greedy we teach prosperity, making the gospel of God's love and fullness into a materialistic orgy of health and wealth.

Whenever we attempt to achieve relevance by distorting the gospel, we also render it ineffective and alienate the very people we are trying to touch with it. It will promise benefits without cost and by doing so never achieve the promise. People will forsake it, disillusioned about God even though they might never have met him.

If all that Christianity offers people is a philosophy of life, it is easy to see why people fall for these attempts. But God did not call us to convince the world of our creed or to conform their lives to our values. He called us to demonstrate to them the truth about himself. He loves them and wants to redeem them from the torment of sin. Then they can choose to believe in him or reject him.

Such a presentation of the gospel requires that we let God live through us in ways which are obvious to the world. They must judge our attempts to be relevant, and I admit that this requires a tenuous balance. By Jesus' example we know that we can associate with sinners in their settings in order to demonstrate the life of Christ. We don't need to be offensive in our dress or demeanor. But wherever we do touch the world, there must be substance beneath our style. That substance is not our theology or our morals but the presence of God.

It is that presence, shining out of our words and actions, that will draw people to him. When you can heal a blind man, set a madman free, or confront a prostitute with the forgiveness of God, you won't need to look like the world to get its attention. You will have it.

Prophetic People

> In our day heaven and earth are on tiptoe waiting for the emerging of a Spirit-led, Spirit-intoxicated, Spirit-empowered people. All of creation watches expectantly for the springing up of a disciplined, freely gathered, martyr people who know in this life the life and power of the kingdom of God. It has happened before, it can happen again.[2]

You can't have a hope like Richard Foster's if you also don't share his assessment.

> Individuals can be found here and there whose hearts burn with divine fire. But they are like flaming torches scattered in the night. As yet there has been no gathering of a people of the Spirit. . . . Our century has yet to see the breaking forth of the apostolic church of the Spirit.[3]

How can he say this despite all our superchurches and renewal movements? Quite simply because it's true. No doubt God has done marvelous things in this century to call people into the fullness of his life and to free them to take his presence to the world. Every time, however, the freshness of renewal easily succumbs to man's efforts to control it, define it, and exploit it through programs and institutions. Like Richard Foster, however, I too am confident that it can still happen, and I'm even more convinced by the rising hunger I find in people who are tired of all the sideshows and want to see Jesus reveal himself to people in the reality of everyday life.

The world has had enough of apathetic Christians who are only interested in their own well-being, of political Christians whose only task is to ram morality down the world's throat, of privileged Christians who strut about with an air of superiority as if they have somehow earned God's blessing. God desires to equip a generation of believers who can be what I call prophetic people.

These are not fortune-tellers, but people able to move out of the safety of church structures and terminology and into one-on-one encounters that bring the reality of Jesus into our starving world.

Howard Snyder in *Liberating the Church* defines something similar as he draws a contrast between church people and kingdom people.

> Church people think about how to get people into the church; kingdom people think about how to get the church into the world. Church people worry that the world might change the church; kingdom people work to see the church change the world.[4]

The apostle Paul was a world-changing believer, and he encouraged us to follow his example. In 1 Corinthians 2 he writes very personally about his methods and motives in ministry, and in so doing he gives us five characteristics of the kind of prophetic people that God is seeking today.

"I came to you."

Prophetic people recognize that the work of God always begins in someone's life where they are. The church cannot afford to carve its niche in the mountain and call the world to come up to it. The incarnation itself demonstrates how God wants us to deal with people. He crawls down into the pit of their own pain and misery, shows them how much he loves them, and offers them his hand to lead them out of the pit into life in Christ.

Can we do less? Incarnational evangelism is becoming a popular term for this important concept. Jesus lives in people, and through them he wants to reveal himself to the world. This happens best not in evangelistic rallies but in the natural encounters of everyday living. People don't have to come to church to be touched, since the church goes to them. The church can then rightfully be more concerned with how believers are being vessels during the week than with how many visitors fill the pews.

Whether at work, school, shopping, or play, we are available to be God's agent to anyone near us. This kind of outreach demands loving each person as an individual and extending to him the heart of God by our attitudes and actions. It also means that we need to be ready to act in the spontaneity of uncontrolled settings. That's what impresses me about the early church: 90 percent of its ministry happened on the street. But today 90 percent happens in our own buildings. No wonder we're not touching the world effectively!

Paul was at home whether he was sharing the life of Jesus with a group of women sitting by a river, with hostile Jews in a synagogue, with philosophers at the Areopagus, or with a Roman court. In fact one of the things that impressed the unbelievers about the early believers was how well they functioned in settings that they were not prepared for. The Sanhedrin was awed by Peter and John's defense because these disciples were not learned men.

"I resolved to know nothing while I was with you except Jesus Christ and him crucified."

Prophetic people are preoccupied with Jesus. Regretfully, Christians often get sidelined by various aspects of the Christian experience. They jump on bandwagons such as spiritual gifts, apologetics, pet theologies, or specific methods of prayer or ministry. Listen to people talk about their churches and you'll usually hear them talk of a particular teacher they enjoy or a particular method of ministry.

Why isn't Jesus the main attraction? Anything in the church should find value only in how it helps people love Jesus and walk in obedience to him. He has granted us access to the Father and sent us the Holy Spirit to make that access real for each of us every day. Though people perceive their needs to be physical or emotional, only this intimacy will satisfy their hunger.

This relationship was forged at the cross, where mercy reigned over judgment. By focusing our message on that mercy we can reach the bruised and hurting with the life of Jesus and can help them find not only forgiveness from sin but cleansing to live free of its bondage.

"I came to you in weakness and fear, and with much trembling."

Prophetic people are of necessity courageous people. They are always going past their own sense of personal ease or competence to obey the Spirit. He wants us to touch the world with his power. This doesn't mean that prophetic people are never afraid; they're always afraid, but they find the courage to obey in spite of their fear.

Relevance is risky business. The opportunities to be taken advantage of, or to get in over your head in your attempts to love people, are always present. Most of the time when I'm sensing God's direction to talk or pray with a certain person, I tremble inside. What if they think I'm crazy? What if I mess it up? The flow of God's Spirit lies beyond our own personal comfort. What Jesus did for us wasn't comfortable, and if we don't risk discomfort ourselves we'll never discover the wealth of God's power or the fruitfulness of incarnational ministry.

"My message and my preaching were not with wise and persuasive words, but with a demonstration of the Spirit's power."

We've already talked about this Scripture and our need to depend on God's power moving through us rather than on our natural abilities. It would have been easy for Paul to go to Corinth staking his success on his vast knowledge, experience, or speaking ability. God wanted him, however, to demonstrate to them the power of his presence, and that's why he needed courage. Power was something he couldn't control and couldn't guarantee. He could only obey and trust.

This same choice now faces me every time I lead worship. I know how to put together a series of songs and exhortations that can inspire people to worship. It's easy to rely on those forms because I and everyone else in the room are comfortable with them, instead of following the Spirit to a more powerful display of his presence. If it were up to me I would never pray for the sick in service because sometimes nothing happens, and I hate to risk that. I like doing what I can control. Anything else puts me on the edge, but here is where we find spiritual power.

"[We have received] the Spirit who is from God, that we may understand what God has freely given us."

Prophetic people are led by the Holy Spirit—not plans, formulas, or learned techniques. Jerry Cook, whose book *Love, Acceptance and Forgiveness* seeks to equip people for this kind of ministry, said it well:

> I want to be prophetic. This means that I should be speaking what God is speaking. The gift of prophecy is the gift of insight. I should be bringing God's insight into situations.[5]

This is the heart of being a prophetic person; we bring God's mind into the very situations in which we are involved. And the only way to do this is to be led by the voice of the Spirit.

Remember Jesus' ministry to the Samaritan woman at the well? By the Spirit he knew that she had been married five times and was now living with yet another man. That knowledge convinced her of God's reality, and she surrendered to him. What a powerful encounter, and one which the Spirit can duplicate through us if we'll listen!

Once as one of our women was shopping in a local mall she was disturbed by continued crying from two infants nearby. Glancing over, she muttered to herself about how incompetent the mother was in disciplining her own kids. As she turned back to her shopping the Spirit impressed her to go over and help.

She did, and the woman accepted, explaining that her children had special problems. Then she began to weep uncontrollably. Her husband had just left her and she had no friends in the area. That led to sharing, prayer, and an exchange of phone numbers for future contact.

Rushing to the hospital one day to pray for a premature baby who was in critical condition with respiratory problems, I was reminded of a similar trip I had made a year-and-a-half earlier. That time a baby was about to be born dead. As I prayed for that baby deep inside a voice told me to stop, that this baby wouldn't be healed. But I still prayed for healing, wanting to be a source of hope and faith to the family. The baby died anyway, and I didn't want to make the mistake again and be a source of unsubstantial hope.

In the car I prayed, "Is there any reason, Father, that you want this baby too?"

"No," resounded in my heart. I met others there and we prayed. Within a matter of hours the situation changed dramatically, and eventually the baby recovered fully.

Paul concludes by saying that God wants us to have the mind of Christ, knowing what he is doing and following his direction. Could we love this world more effectively in any other way?

People of Power

This kind of ministry is not for people who are pressed by guilt or the need to validate their salvation by works. We waste countless dollars, energy, and time trying to motivate people to evangelism. What a contrast that is from Peter's words, when all the effort of his day was being used to stop the early Christians from sharing their faith: "We cannot help speaking about what we have seen and heard" (Acts 4:20).

Evangelism in the early church was not submission to a difficult obedience. It was as natural for the early believers to talk about God as it is for us to talk about a football game when our team defeats an archrival in the last second. We talk about it with close friends and even work it into conversations with clerks in stores and strangers in lines. We relive the excitement every time in the retelling.

Unfortunately, for too many Christians the life of Jesus is not as correspondingly exciting. So we think we have to force people to talk about Jesus, even though such sharing is canned and forced. That's not what Peter and John were doing at the temple; they couldn't stop themselves. A lame man had been healed and people were asking questions—no contrived dialogue here! Their faith was really exciting enough to compete with new houses and Olympic games, and people wanted to listen.

The reason many people are not interested in the gospel is that they heard about it from someone who either wasn't living it or was finding no joy in doing so. No amount of contrived joy or institutional program will remedy the problem; intimacy must precede any valid work of evangelism. If it's not real for us, how can we convey its reality to someone else?

This is true for each believer as well as for the church as a whole. Every church should be challenged by David Watson's words:

> Until the kingdom of God can be demonstrated in our relationships of love with one another, we will have nothing credible to say to an unbelieving world.[6]

On the day he ascended, Jesus told his disciples to go back to Jerusalem and wait until they were filled with power. That's good advice for us. If Jesus isn't alive in you, that must be your only priority. Learn to be filled with his presence; then, like the disciples, you will find yourself being a witness. It isn't something you have to force.

When he's not that real for us, it's a warning sign to deepen or rebuild our relationship with him. There are many ways to do this, such as fasting, having extended times of prayer, or seeking the counsel of another believer. The reasons these are so unused today is that we really aren't looking for God's presence to be demonstrated through us. If God's presence isn't the goal of those things, then we'll find them to be ineffective in accomplishing whatever else we want to do.

But if we want God to be alive in us, to meet our needs as well as those of others, then fasting becomes a useful tool to suppress the aggressiveness of the flesh and bask in God's presence. Worship and prayer become effective links to God's heart. Our need for the support, encouragement, and friendship of other believers will be undeniable.

Wait on him until his presence becomes a reality, until his power courses through your veins. Then you're ready to be a vessel wherever you are and with all the resources which the Spirit has to share through you.

The Harvest Is Ready

Even in the self-sufficiency of Western culture, Jesus' words are still true: "The harvest is plentiful." If we can look past the facades that our world uses to hide its pain, maybe we can see what Mother Teresa sees:

> The spiritual poverty of the Western world is much greater than the physical poverty of our people. You in the West have millions of people who suffer such terrible loneliness and emptiness.[7]

It is also true that the "workers are few." Extending the reality of God's kingdom is the only reason we still exist on this planet, and the spreading of that message to more people is the only reason God delays to send his Son back again for us.

If God's only objective is for us to have closer fellowship with him, he might as well kill us at conversion. No matter how closely we walk with him in this life, it is but a shadow of what we will know of him throughout eternity. We are here so that others might see him in us. None of us can escape that call, but if you're growing in intimacy you won't want to.

The church of Jesus Christ is an underground movement in occupied land. Our joy will be found only in fulfilling the mission that God has given us. Dietrich Bonhoeffer was a brilliant young theologian in Germany. During World War II his friends smuggled him out of Germany to save his life, only to see him give up his newfound freedom and willingly return. "I shall have no right to participate in the reconstruction of Christian life in Germany after the war if I do not share the trials for this time with my people."[8]

He died in a German prison camp only days before it was liberated by the Allies. His words should carry great weight when he wrote:

> The church must get out of the cloister and into the world . . . [where] man is challenged to participate in the sufferings of God at the hands of a godless world. He must therefore plunge himself into the life of a godless world without attempting to gloss over its ungodliness with a veneer of religion or trying to transfigure it. He must live a worldly life and so participate in the suffering of God.[9]

Bringing God's goodness to a world that prefers its own selfishness isn't easy. But when we are full of God's power we will do so with a depth of compassion that flows even to those who work hardest against us. Then Jesus will show himself through our lives in situations that we would never choose and ways that we would never expect.

It is a mystery of profound consequence that God can encase his glory in earthen vessels!

21

From Glory to Glory: The Road Ahead

We, who with unveiled faces
all reflect the Lord's glory,
are being transformed into his likeness
with ever-increasing glory.
—2 Corinthians 3:18

The road that will lead you to a full, intimate friendship with God lies beneath your feet and unfolds before you as it winds into hills and valleys yet unknown. Though you cannot see what circumstances it will traverse, you can rest secure that it promises to reveal God's presence in your life with ever-increasing glory.

Discovering the depths of friendship with God is an invitation to a life-long adventure, full of wonder and intrigue. You may not be able to see far down the road, but now it is enough for you to take only the next step God asks of you. I trust that will be clear enough to you after reading this book.

Make sure that this step and every ensuing one are measured to take you closer to God. Nourish your passion for His presence, for the road to intimacy is not the only path at your feet. As we've seen throughout this book, there are others intended to lead you astray.

It is always your choice which you will take. I'll not pretend that the road to intimacy will always look the easiest or the most rewarding. But the seeming lack of reward is only a deception. Your flesh is certain to complain, but no one has ever undertaken this journey who was disappointed with its joys.

And as for not looking easy—that part is true. Though we know what lies at the end of the road to intimacy, there's no way to guess the twists and turns it will take to get us there

Dangers abound, and the risk to our own personal safety is great. The road to God's heart winds through a battlefield, where casualties need healing and other soldiers a helping hand. The outcome of the battles we'll face holds in the balance no less a prize than the redemption of people from the tyranny of evil.

But don't confuse the battle with the road. Our destination is not a battlefield but the throne room of God. Though we fully arrive there at the end, every day we can partake of the firstfruits of that final redemption. For God does not merely wait for us at its end, but comes alongside us to share the journey. He invites us to intimacy, a real fellowship that not only inspires us but transforms us into his likeness. "With ever-increasing glory" is how he describes it, for here is joy and beauty beyond our wildest imagining. It is an adventure for a lifetime. We will never in this life (or in eternity) probe all the depths of God's goodness and grace.

There is nothing left to say except to invite you to come. Over the course of these pages we've looked at the depth of relationship that God wants for us. Though we've looked at a lot of things in Western Christianity that fall short of what God has called us to, my intent was not to breed controversy or to stimulate intellectual curiosity. It was only to show how we've been willingly duped because we hold a vested interest in its failures.

Though the terms I've used have been clearly distinguishable hues of black and white, I've done so only to make the grays more visible. The shades of compromise are the most deceptive. We all find ways to fit our own desires to religious forms, giving us the pretense of safety but not its reality. Ask Jesus to show you what distracts you from the relationship with him that he wants.

I've not wanted to breed cynics who can only jeer from the sidelines, and that is why the solution I've given has been personal. This is not to say that I don't think the structures should be changed, for they harm many sincere believers as well as alienate many nonbelievers. It's just that few who read this book will have the power to change structures.

If you do, by all means lend your voice to a call for repentance. I've no doubt that Jesus will judge the Western church for its abuses and excesses, and in fact has already begun to do so. We, like the people of Jesus' day, might prefer him to march into Pilate's court and upset the wicked secularists, but instead he marches to the temple to throw out those who have made a mockery of his work.

Don't be dismayed when future revelations bring down those you thought you could trust, or when institutions fail you. God wants to turn our hearts back to him without anyone standing in the way. What he offers you—intimacy with him— can apply to your life without changing one structure around you. And if enough people do that, we might just be contagious enough to convince the Emperor to put his clothes back on.

But whether he does or not, make sure *you* do. Jesus warned us not to be caught naked on the day of his appearing:

> Behold, I come like a thief! Blessed is he who stays awake and keeps his clothes with him, so that he may not go naked and be shamefully exposed (Revelation 16:15).

Don't put this book away until you've decided to give your relationship with Jesus the highest priority. Every day set aside time to be in his presence in worship and study of the Word. Listen to him and submit to whatever he tells you. Find a group of believers who desire God's presence and are not just trying to fill their time with religious activity.

Keep hungering for God, refusing to be satisfied until the reality of his life in you matches the promises of his Word. You have to be aggressive, pursuing with eager feet, for the enemies are many who will seek to stop you.

This is a battlefield like none other: The real enemies aren't visible; the casualties are not obvious; good ideas can be as destructive as wicked deeds.

You'll face the enemy of your own flesh, which prefers temporal comforts to the cost of intimacy. You'll face the preoccupations of the institutional church itself, which prefers its own survival to being flexible to the breath of the Spirit. You'll face the enemy himself, who seeks to devour and destroy you by hurling discouragement, temptation, and discomfort at your every attempt toward intimacy with God.

None of these enemies, however, are bigger than our God, and if you persevere in your relationship with him there will be no enemy able to stop you from enjoying the fullness of God's life.

Knowing God personally is not too difficult for anyone who wants it. We ourselves can do so little to build intimacy, for God himself is too good at it. We can only allow ourselves to be distracted from it. But even when we do, we must not let even our own failures thwart our pursuit.

Jesus does not demand perfection from us, and we must not do so of ourselves or others. Even before Peter denied him, Jesus looked past his failure and encouraged him to pick himself up and come back to minister to the other disciples. Jesus knows that the strength of the flesh will at times make us do what he and we both know is not in our heart to do. For that there is forgiveness and a chance to start fresh every day. He will transform you as you keep coming to him with an open heart.

Why don't you come? When you taste the reality of God's presence and feel his robe of righteousness slip around your shoulders, you'll have no doubt that it is all worth it. For then we can be the people of God in this age, taking his power to the agony of our world.

There are still sick people to be healed, outcasts to be loved, captives to be freed—and people poor of possession and spirit to be filled with God's life.

God wants you to help him do it. You will, won't you?

NOTES

Chapter 2—Rise Up and Walk?
1. "How Does Ronald Reagan Stand on the Issues?" in *Charisma*, Oct. 1984, p. 180.
2. Gallup-Schuller Poll, 1982.
3. "How Religious Are We?" A Reader's Digest-Gallup Poll (*Reader's Digest*, May 1986), p. 102.
4. J. David Schmidt, "How to Raise a Billion Dollars," *Christianity Today*, May 15, 1987, p. 36.
5. Richard Ostling, "Enterprising Evangelists," *Time*, Aug. 3, 1987, pp. 38-41.
6. "Yearbook of American and Canadian Churches," 1983. Compiled by the National Council of Churches and reported in the *Visalia Times-Delta*, Jul. 16, 1983.
7. "Amsterdam Reports" (*Ministries*, Fall 1983).
8. Chuck Colson, *Loving God* (Zondervan, 1983), p. 14.
9. Beth Spring, "A Gallup Poll Finds a Rising Tide of Interest In Religion," in *Christianity Today*, Oct. 21, 1983, p. 41.
10. "Less Pressure, More Loving," interview with Jerry Cook in *Leadership*, Spring 1984.
11. Chuck Colson, "Jesus Is Lord," in *Charisma*, May 1985.
12. From the Epilogue of *Experiencing the Depths of Jesus Christ*, by Madame Guyon (Christian Books, 1980).
13. Rodney Clapp, "Looking From the Downside Up, An interview with Walter Wangerin, Jr." in *Christianity Today*, Mar. 1, 1985, p. 19.
14. David Watson, *Called and Committed* (Harold Shaw, 1982), p. 32.
15. As told to Cornelius a Lapide and quoted by F. F. Bruce in *The New International Commentary—The Book of Acts* (Eerdman's Publishing Company, 1974), p. 84.
16. Chuck Colson, "Speaking for God," in *Eternity*, Apr. 1984, p. 40.
17. Howard Snyder, *Liberating the Church* (InterVarsity Press, 1983), p. 149.
18. Peter Marshall and David Manuel, *The Light and the Glory* (Revell, 1977), p. 249.

Chapter 3—The Emperor's New Clothes
1. *A Manifesto for the Christian Church*, copyright 1986. Used with the permission of the Coalition on Revival, Dr. Jay Grimstead, Director, 89 Pioneer Way, Mountain View, CA 94041.

Chapter 4—Aren't You Hungry?
1. Charles Finney, *Revival Lectures* (Revell, n.d.), p. 29.
2. Ibid., p. 7.
3. Roland H. Bainton, *Here I Stand* (Festival Books, 1950).
4. Sheldon Vanauken, *Under the Mercy* (Thomas Nelson, 1985), p. 106.
5. Interview with Os Guiness in *Eternity*, Sep. 1983, p. 26.

Chapter 5—Of Course I Love God!
1. "Reflections," in *Christianity Today*, Dec. 13, 1985, p. 46.
2. Walter Wangerin, Jr., *The Ragman and Other Cries of Faith* (Harper and Row, 1984), p. 73.
3. Ibid., p. 75.
4. "An Interview with David Duplessis," in *Charisma*, May 1985, p. 56.
5. Em Griffin, "Four Ways to Make Group Decisions," in *Leadership*, Spring 1982, pp. 74-82.
6. Richard Foster, *Celebration of Discipline* (Harper and Row, 1978), p. 33.

Chapter 6—Real Salvation
1. *Visalia Times-Delta*, Jul. 17, 1985.
2. C. Peter Wagner, *Leading Your Church to Growth* (Regal, 1984), p. 56.
3. Ward Gasque, "Most Ordinary People Know Theology," in *Christianity Today*, Feb. 1, 1985, p. 33.
4. Colson, *Loving God*, p. 95.

Chapter 7—When Did It Get So Complicated?
1. Wagner, *Leading*, p. 49.
2. Charles Finney, *Revival Lectures* (Revell, n.d.), p. 41.

Chapter 8—Simple Intimacy
1. Tim Stafford, *Knowing the Face of God* (Zondervan, 1976), p. 23.
2. C. Peter Wagner, *Your Spiritual Gifts Can Help Your Church Grow* (Regal, 1976), p. 32 (as quoted by John Wimber in *Power Evangelism*).
3. Stafford, *Knowing*, p. 187.
4. Wangerin, *Ragman*, p. 85.
5. Finney, *Revival*, p. 53.

Chapter 9—God in a Box
1. Wangerin, *Ragman*, p. 73.
2. Interview, "A Scientist Caught Between Two Faiths," in *Christianity Today*, Aug. 6, 1982, p. 15.
3. Ibid.
4. Quoted in *Leadership*, Winter 1986, p. 79.
5. Robert Schuller, *Hope for Tough Times*.
6. Snyder, *Liberating*, p. 163.
7. C. S. Lewis, *The Problem of Pain*, p. 128.

Chapter 10—Intimacy and Dependency
1. Finney, *Revival*, p. 124.
2. An Interview with Gordon MacDonald, Robert M. Kachur, and David Neff in *Christianity Today*, Apr. 18, 1986, p. 22.
3. Andrew Murray, *Waiting on God* (Christian Literature Crusade, 1978), p. 26.

Chapter 11—Golden Shepherds
1. Robert C. Girard, *Brethren, Hang Together* (Zondervan, 1979), p. 208.
2. Colson, *Loving God*, p. 14.

Chapter 12—Intimacy and Accountability
1. Howard A. Snyder, *The Community of the King* (InterVarsity Press, 1978), pp. 94-95.
2. Watson, *Called*, p. 47.
3. Frederick Buechner, "Telling The Truth," in *Leadership*, Winter 1984, pp. 24-25.

Chapter 13—Confessions of a Christian Materialist
1. Johannes Jorgensen, *St. Francis of Assisi* (Image Books, 1912), p. 49.
2. Marilyn Hickey, "Get Your Mind in Line," in *Charisma*, Jun. 1986, p. 15.
3. Edmund K. Gravely, "Dave Wilkerson," in *Charisma*, Sep. 1983.
4. Foster, *Celebration*, p. 71.
5. "Publishers Watch Book Trends," in *Charisma*, Apr. 1982, p. 42.
6. James and Elizabeth Newby, "An Interview with Malcolm Muggeridge," in *Eternity*, Apr. 1984, p. 27.
7. Foster, *Celebration*, p. 70.
8. James Dobson, "Turn Your Heart Toward Home" (film series).

Chapter 14—The Righteousness That Comes from Faith
1. Foster, *Celebration*, pp. 5-6.
2. "Less Pressure, More Loving," interview with Jerry Cook in *Leadership*, Spring 1984.

Chapter 15—Programmed to Death
1. With a tip of the hat to C. S. Lewis, author of *The Screwtape Letters*.
2. Frank Herbert, *Dune Messiah* (Berkley Books, 1984), pp. 178-179.
3. Snyder, *Liberating*, p. 20.
4. Charles Hummel, "In Search for the One Best Way," in *Pastoral Renewal*, Jan. 1984.
5. Snyder, *Community*, p. 67.
6. "How to Grow a Church," in *Ministries*, Spring 1983, p. 37.
7. Ibid.
8. Os Guiness, interview in *Eternity*, Sep. 1983.
9. Frank Herbert, *Children of Dune* (Berkley Books, 1981), p. 224.

Chapter 16—The New Testament Community
1. Watson, *Called*, p. 17.
2. Stephen Strang, "Dr. Cho Talks About Cell Groups," in *Ministries*, Spring 1983, p. 31.
3. Watson, *Called*, p. 24.
4. Arthur Blessitt, *Arthur, A Pilgrim* (Blessitt Publishing, 1985), p. 338.
5. Girard, *Hang Together*, p. 29.
6. Watson, *Called*, p. 31.

Chapter 17—Where Has All the Power Gone?
1. Harold S. Kushner, *When Bad Things Happen to Good People* (Avon, 1981), p. 114.
2. Susan Holt Porter, "My Angry Son," in *Reader's Digest*, Feb. 1984.
3. Dave Hunt, *Beyond Seduction* (Harvest House, 1987), pp. 73-74.
4. Tim Stafford, "Testing the Wine from John Wimber's Vineyard," in *Christianity Today*, Aug. 8, 1986, p. 22.
5. Ibid.
6. Ibid.

Chapter 18—Clothed with Power
1. Todd Burke, *Anointed for Burial* (Logos), p. 216.
2. Lloyd John Ogilvie, *The Autobiography of God* (Regal Books, 1979), p. 72.

Chapter 19—Stained Glass and White Linen
1. Interview with Os Guiness in *Eternity*, Sep. 1983.
2. James L. Johnson, *Codename: Sebastian* (Lippincott, 1967).
3. Quoted by Jerry Cook in *Love, Acceptance and Forgiveness* (Regal, 1979), p. 44.
4. Colson, *Loving God*, p. 192.
5. Ibid.
6. Herbert, *Children*, p. 225.
7. Colson, *Loving God*, p. 192.

Chapter 20—A Real Jesus in an Unreal World
1. Johnson, *Codename*.
2. Foster, *Celebration*, p. 150.
3. Ibid.
4. Snyder, *Liberating*.
5. Jerry Cook, *Love, Acceptance and Forgiveness* (Regal, 1979), p. 27.
6. Watson, *Called*, p. 20.
7. Quoted in *Leadership*, Winter 1987, p. 35.
8. From the Memoir in the second edition of *The Cost of Discipleship*, by G. Leibholz (MacMillan, 1979), p. 16.
9. Johnson, *Codename*.